THE MASSACRE OF GLENCOE

THE MASSACRE OF GLENCOE

BY

JOHN BUCHAN

BUCHAN & ENRIGHT, PUBLISHERS
London

First published in 1933 by Peter Davies Ltd.

This edition first published in 1985 by
Buchan & Enright, Publishers, Limited
53 Fleet Street, London EC4Y 1BE

British Library Cataloguing in Publication Data
Buchan, John, *1875–1940*
The massacre of Glencoe. — (Echoes of war)
1. Glencoe Massacre, 1692
I. Title   II. Series
941.106'8   DA804.7

ISBN 0–907675–41–7

Printed in Great Britain by
Redwood Burn Limited, Trowbridge, Wiltshire
and bound by Pegasus Bookbinding, Melksham, Wiltshire

ALICIAE
FILIOLAE
DILECTISSIMAE

NOTE

In this essay in reconstruction I have tried
to include no detail which has not a warrant
from contemporary evidence, or is not a
legitimate deduction from such evidence.
The only liberty I have taken is now and
then to state boldly as a fact what should
strictly be qualified by a ' probably.'

J. B.

CONTENTS

ILLUSTRATIONS

13

CHAPTER I

THE FORT OF INVERLOCHY

THE Governor's room in the fort was a cheer-less place on that afternoon of late December. It was barely furnished; a couple of travelling-chests, a big deal table crowded with papers, one or two chairs of local make with seats of untanned hide, and a camp bed in a corner. On the floor were skins of deer, and on one wall a stand of arms. The peat fire was burn-ing badly, as it always did in a north-west wind, and the blue smoke from it clouded without warming the air. The small windows were plastered with drifting snow. The man who sat writing at the table stopped to listen to the gale, which howled outside and deadened the tramp of the sentry's feet. He shivered, and turned up the collar of his military greatcoat.

Colonel John Hill was an old man, well on in the sixties, with a lean tired face and washed-out eyes. He held himself erect, but rheumatism crippled his movements. That spring he had been sick for three months with fever and ague, and, though his health had improved in the summer, the wet autumn had brought a relapse and he had felt strangely inert and vigourless. Moreover, at no time in his long career had he been so cumbered with perplexities. He had got little out of life, and now the burden of it was becoming too heavy for him. Long ago he had lost all ambition and asked only for peace and a modest comfort, but these blessings were still denied him.

He took from a file a copy of the letter he had written to Lord Tarbat eight months before —Tarbat had always been his friend. 'I find illwishers grow upon me,' he read, ' and some great men. They say I am old, and would, I think, have me to reduce all the Highlands myself, which, if I could do, there would be as little need for them as there is for this garrison. I would his Majesty would give me any other place where I could be serviceable to him, and let some emulators take this, and then I might be quiet.' That plaint reminded him of the Psalms of David and he muttered a verse or two to himself. He had always been a religious man.

The weather matched his mood. He let his pen drop, sank his chin into his greatcoat, and permitted his mind to run over his past vicissitudes and present distractions. For forty years and more he had been a soldier. Long ago in Cromwell's day he had served under George Monk in Fitch's regiment, and had come from Ruthven to command in this very fort of Inverlochy which Monk had built to bridle the wild Highlandmen. He had been young then and had loved the service, and the great Duke of Albemarle was a leader he had been proud to follow. He himself had been popular with the natives, and had hunted and fished with the chiefs ; many a gift of salmon and venison had reached him from the hills ; he had proclaimed Richard Cromwell in the market-place in the presence of Lochiel and Glengarry, and when King Charles came back to his own he had surrendered Inverlochy to Lochiel in all friendliness. He was a soldier, and knew no politics.

Since then he had heard the drum in various quarters of the world, but hc had always

B   17

cherished happy memories of Scotland. He had corresponded with the old laird of Culloden and with his son Duncan, the present laird, and he had now Duncan's brother John as his major. When the Revolution came he had been Constable of Belfast Castle and had made a stout stand against the Irish rebels ; but for him, he believed the victory of the Boyne would not have been achieved. His reward had been to be sent to Scotland in June 1690, to take over the Inverlochy garrison which General Hugh Mackay had revived on Monk's plan.

There had been trouble from the first. Mackay, whose temper had not been improved by Killiecrankie, was captious, vain and irritable, with none of Monk's calm supremacy. The Jacobite commander-in-chief, Thomas Buchan, had indeed been soundly beaten by Sir Thomas Livingstone at Cromdale, and had since been vainly attempting what Mackay called the ' chicane ' of war in Aberdeenshire, but it had been feared that any day he might come west to trouble Lochaber. Hill had felt himself called to too arduous a service. Scotland was a bleak place for a man who was in

failing health and growing old. He considered
that he deserved more comfortable rewards.
The knighthood which was his due still tarried.
He wanted a pension. He wanted a good regiment, and had only got an amalgam of the
weak remnants of Kenmure's and Glencairn's.
Above all he wanted to be paid monies due to
him. All his life he had been spending out of
his own pocket on the public service : on pro-
viding a minister's stipend in the days of Cromwell ; on garrisoning Belfast ; and now on
finding Inverlochy in the bare necessaries of
life and defence.

His one pride was this fort of his, for of the
policy which it exemplified he had been the
chief begetter, and it carried the memories of
his far-away youth. It had been christened
Fort William, and the new works had been
erected in eleven days. Mackay had found
fault with the old site in the angle of the river
Nevis, on the plea that it could be commanded
from higher ground—as if the clans had much
artillery ! But he had made a solid business
of the defence—fosse, wall twenty feet high
palisaded around, *glacis* and *chemin couvert*. The
chief trouble had been the barracks inside for

the garrison of more than a thousand men, for no wood could be got in that countryside of scrub birch and hazel, and the Government were unconscionably slow in sending timber from Leith and the Clyde. Every week he had to write to Melville or Tarbat or Livingstone pleading for supplies.

It was not Mackay's blame. Before he left the Scottish command he had written to the Duke of Hamilton—Hill had seen the letter—declaring that the Inverlochy fort was 'the most important of the kingdom at present, and that which will at length make such as would sell their credit or service at such a dear rate to the King of no greater use, nor more necessary to him, than a Lothian or Fife laird,' and urging that 'it be by no means neglected though other things should be postponed.' But supplies still came laggardly. The garrison was short of ammunition, ill-clad and ill-shod; it was provisioned from Argyll and Kintyre, but food was constantly running low, and the men's rations were often only meal and water and a tot of *aqua vitae*. Small wonder that their temper was getting ugly.

VIEW OF GLENCOE

Photo by Judges' Ltd.

There had been other troubles, some of them happily past. The first garrison had been four companies of the Angus regiment, four of Argyll's, and nine of the laird of Grant's. The Angus men, and especially their chaplain, did not like the place, and they had been sent to Flanders ; Hill had regretted it, for they were good soldiers. After that he had been left with Grant's and Argyll's, and now they were all Argyll's. These last were Highlanders, and he was a little doubtful whether hawks could be trusted to pick out hawks' eyes. Angus's whiggamores were a troublesome folk, but more dependable. Then there was the question of a deputy-governor and lieutenant-colonel for the garrison. He refused to have a Highlander, and in the end got a certain James Hamilton, a Lowlander with good connections—a competent man, but a difficult subordinate, for he was in private correspondence with Sir John Dalrymple, the Secretary for Scotland, and Livingstone, who had succeeded Mackay as commander-in-chief, wrote to him more often than to the Governor.

Lastly, there was the eternal anxiety about communications. There were three routes to Inverlochy : one by sea from the south, and two by land. Of the land routes, that from Inverness had to pass through Glengarry's country, and that from Atholl through Badenoch was commanded by Keppoch, and in any case was not open till the middle of June. The only safe communication was by water. But the Government showed no sense of the importance of the sea route, they sent too few frigates and kept up no regular system of supply. Yet Lochaber was a powder magazine, a turn of fortune's wheel on the Continent and French ships of war would be off its coast, Buchan and the other Jacobite leaders were still at large. Hill never sent out his patrols into Brae Lochaber or west into the Rough Bounds without a fear lest they should bring back news that the fiery cross had gone round and that the heather was ablaze.

He disliked politics, but he had perforce to take a hand in them, and a fine confusion they presented to a simple fighting man. At the head of all was William, a great king and a fine soldier whom Hill revered ; but how could

one who had just finished a stiff campaign in
Ireland, and was now engaged in a life-and-
death struggle in Flanders, spare time for the
affairs of this distant northern land ? Yet
William had recognised the merits of the Inverlochy scheme ; a namesake of Hill's own, a
captain of Leven's, had seen him at Chester on
the matter nineteen months ago, and the King
had peremptorily ordered the Council to supply
anything needed for the work. That was well
enough, but the King's vicegerents in Scotland had no such clearness of purpose. To
a plain soldier like himself they seemed to be
concerned more about their personal aggran-
disement than about the peace of the realm,
and to rate the settlement of their Kirk
higher than the pacification of Scotland. He
was a devout man, but he had no patience
with their religious bickerings. The fortunes
of the land were on a razor's edge, and those
lawyer folk would not see it. They squabbled
about their family interests, when a single
reverse to British arms on the Continent might
stir the Highlands and send down on the
Lowlands a spate of desperate men.

There was Melville, with his big head and

ashen face and mean presence, who thought
more of advancing his son Leven's career than
of soldierly measures of defence. A Presbyterian of the old rock and no doubt an honest
man, but a slow and tortuous one. There was
Tarbat, handsome and genial, but slippery like
all of the Mackenzie blood. And now there
was the Master of Stair, another lawyer, who
was said to hold the chief place in the King's
confidence. Hill had never met him, but he
had heard much about the Dalrymples. His
mother was said to have been a witch, and the
old Viscount, his father, was reputed the
craftiest brain in the kingdom. Sir John,
now Master of Stair, was one of the new
Secretaries of State ; he was hated by the
Presbyterians for having been King's advocate
under James, and by the Jacobites for having
shamelessly turned his coat. No man had ever
in his hearing said a good word for Sir John,
but all had spoken with solemnity of his
devilish subtlety and cold relentlessness of
purpose. But even if these civilians meant
honestly, they were hampered by utter ignor-
ance of the Highlander. Tarbat was different;
he knew his own race, and Hill had found him

25

the easiest to work with. The others were Lowlanders, knowing less of the Gael than Hill knew of the Kamchatkans, but with an ancestral hatred and distrust of all who wore tartan. There were indeed two Highlanders who had the knowledge, but they were scarcely men to ride the ford with. There was Argyll, who had offered to serve against his own father and for whom none had a kind word. And there was Breadalbane.

The last was the personage who for the past twelve months had been giving Hill his most anxious thoughts. He had known him of old, and trusted him not at all. No one living had had a stranger career, for this Highland chief had made himself great and rich by a combination of the methods of attorney and cateran. As Sir John Campbell of Glenorchy he had lent money to the bankrupt Earl of Caithness, and foreclosed on his title and estates ; he had fought a battle at Wick to establish his claim ; being deprived of the title he had won as mortgagee, he had got a new patent as Earl of Breadalbane ; he had extended his territory from Loch Awe to Loch Tay by beggaring his neighbours ; he had been deep in every

26

Jacobite plot, and yet he had some inexplicable secret influence at William's court. Next to Argyll he was the most powerful man in the Highlands, but he was less disliked than Argyll, for he had a certain surface geniality. His avarice was notorious, but he could be friendly when it cost him nothing. Mackay had hated him, and Mackay for all his megrims was an acute judge of character.

Breadalbane had no love for Inverlochy, for he had a scheme of his own—that the Government should make it worth the while of the chiefs to submit and live at peace. This was a popular policy among the Scottish statesmen of Highland blood, for each wanted to be chosen as intermediary, since doubtless there would be pickings in the business. There was sense in the proposal, Hill thought, if it were adopted side by side with his own and Mackay's scheme of forts and garrisons. Some of the money allotted might be used to buy up the disputed feudal superiorities which were a sore point with the clans ; Argyll, for example, had certain claims to superiority over Macdonald lands, and there could be no peace till that thorn was plucked out. Hill himself had been

27

inclined to make the attempt when he first came to Scotland, the efforts of Campbell of Cawdor having failed, and he had spent some weary weeks travelling the Highlands without success. The sum named was too small, only £2000, and the proffered peerages found no acceptors. Hill's reason assented to the plan, but his instincts were against it, and he feared its maleficent extension. The time had not yet come to trust the Highlanders ; a just and firm policy was the immediate need. A wise man like Duncan Forbes of Culloden saw this, and he was as good a Highlander as Breadalbane, who wanted to turn the clans into a standing army in Government pay.

Eight months ago the financial scheme had been revived. There had been some curious by-play about the business at which he could only guess, for the chiefs themselves had been sounded as to the best negotiator. None would accept Argyll ; Glengarry had wanted Atholl ; but Lochiel had been strong for his cousin Breadalbane, and Breadalbane had been chosen. There had been a moment in the previous spring when the Government had leaned to severity, and he had been ordered by

SIR EWEN CAMERON OF LOCHIEL

(*From the portrait by an unknown artist in the Scottish National
Portrait Gallery*)

the Council forthwith to summon and disarm
the clans and compel an oath of submission at
the point of the sword. The order had been
insane and he had protested, but he had duly
issued the summons, and found that the
' middle sort of people ' everywhere were
ready to submit. Lochiel, Keppoch, Clanranald, the Macleans and the Macintoshes,
the men of Appin and Glencoe, all seemed to
be in a yielding humour ; only Sleat and
Glengarry were refractory, and the latter had
set about fortifying his house.

But presently he heard that the order was
rescinded, and that Breadalbane was busy with
his diplomacy. In the last days of June there
was a conference at his castle of Achallader,
which looked over Loch Tulla from under the
shadow of the Glenlyon hills. Many of the
chiefs were present, and the Jacobite leaders,
Buchan and Barclay, and there a truce was
signed to last till October 1. During that
period there were to be no acts of hostility by
either side on land or sea. There were also
certain secret articles which provided that the
truce was only to hold if James approved, and
if there was no general rising, and that, if it

fell through, Breadalbane was to rise for James
with a thousand men.

Hill had got wind of the secret clauses and
had duly sent them to Sir Thomas Livingstone,
his official chief, while the Council received
another copy from a nephew of Buchan. The
result had been a furious row with Breadalbane,
who was sore also at the failure of his bribery
scheme. With that he had made no headway.
The chiefs would not submit to be patronised
by one whom they considered no better than
themselves, and they distrusted his promises,
believing that the London gold would never
get beyond the vaults of Kilchurn. Hill's
conscience in the matter was clear. Much as
he disliked Breadalbane, he had done his best
to help him, and had laboured to persuade
Keppoch and Lochiel. But meantime the
Government had followed up the Achallader
truce. On the 27th of August 1691, there was
issued at Edinburgh a proclamation pardoning
and indemnifying all who had been in arms
against the Government, provided that, before
the first day of January 1692, they took the oath
of allegiance before a sheriff or sheriff-depute.

Hill had not been fully convinced of the

wisdom of the step. To ask within a period of
five months the disavowal of the politics of a
lifetime was to ask a good deal. He would have
preferred to let Jacobitism as a sentiment die
slowly away, but to keep a strict check on its
armed manifestations. But his duty was to
obey, and at any rate the Government seemed
to have got a new vigour. Recalcitrants were
to be firmly dealt with, and the regiments of
Leven and of Buchan's Whig brother John were
ordered to be ready for action.

At first he had been hopeful. In May there
had been, as he had reported, a very genuine
desire on the part of the clans to come in,
except a few hot-heads. The Appin and
Glencoe men had been willing to go to Inveraray, and take the oath before Argyll, their
feudal superior, a marvellous concession for
two most turbulent septs. Achtriachtan, one
of the cadet gentry of Glencoe, and the tacksman of Inverrigan had made their submission
and been given his protection early in Nov-
ember. The Government had been discreet,
and had been faithful to the ' gentle methods '
which he had recommended. He had had
trouble with Stewart of Appin, who had im-

prisoned one of his soldiers, and he had been compelled to arrest him and a son of Glencoe and bring them to Inverlochy, but they had been released on the Queen's special order.

But as the months passed he had been growing anxious. The honour of the Highlander had been touched, and no man would take the lead in renouncing ancient loyalties, especially as there were constant rumours of French fleets on the sea and of King James returning to his own. He had expected trouble with Sleat and the contumacious Glengarry, but the whole Highlands seemed to be recusant. It was now almost the end of December and few clans had come in. Lochiel, Glengarry, Keppoch, Appin had not sworn, and only a day or two remained. . . . That morning he had had word that Lochiel was starting for Inveraray. It was like the crooked Highland mind to deem it more honourable to postpone to the last moment an inevitable step.

Hill rose and walked to the window on the side away from the wind. The snow had stopped drifting, and the last gleam of daylight revealed beyond a rampart a shoulder of hill,

a strip of leaden loch, and a low sullen sky.
He shivered. There were months yet of winter
before him, and his ague would assuredly
return. What a God-forgotten country, and
what a cruel fate for an old man to be mar-
ooned among these wilds ! He thought of his
daughters in London whom he never saw ; he
should be in the bosom of a family at his
age, with a knighthood and a pension and
a sinecure, instead of dwelling cold in the
wilderness. . . .

And then—for the man's mind was just—
he was a little ashamed of his humour. After
all, he had position and respect, a roof to cover
him and food to eat, which was more than
could be said of some of James's men who had
embraced beggary for a scruple. It was more
than could be said of most of the clans, who
every winter were on the verge of starvation.
All round him the common folk looked white
and peaked. To send soldiers, who had a
bellyful of meat under their belts, against such
scarecrows was scarcely decent. . . . To his
surprise, as he looked over the darkening
narrows of Loch Linnhe, he found himself a
partisan of the Highlanders.

34

The truth was that he liked them, as Mackay had liked them. Mackay had always said that they were the best natural material for soldiers on earth, and he agreed with him. That made them a peril to the State, but some day it might make them a shining buckler. They had done famously at Killiecrankie, and at the worst they had been true to their salt. Moreover, they were friendly folk and well-mannered, and when they spoke English at all they spoke it intelligibly, and not like Angus's whiggamores, whom he had found wholly incomprehensible. They were noble companions in the chase or over a friendly bottle. For some of them, like Lochiel, he had a warm affection. Besides, he felt himself called on to be their protector, for had he not known them for nearly forty years ? His policy was Monk's rather than Mackay's ; Monk had believed in a firm policing hand and with it patience, while Mackay had wanted to set a date for surrender and after that ' to rouse them out of the nation as the bane thereof.' He did not like that kind of language, though by it Mackay only meant burning their houses and crops ; it was too like Breadalbane's talk of ' mauling ' them, which he suspected had a

35

more sinister implication than Mackay's. The worst enemy of the Highlander might be other Highlanders.

Suppose their recalcitrance continued beyond the appointed day. Then there would be ugly work, since the troops would be loosed among the winter hills. There would be beyond question barbarities, and he was less afraid of Leven's and Buchan's Lowlanders than of his own men of Argyll's. In his recent letters there had been talk of extirpation, an ominous word. He comforted himself by reflecting that a great clan, like the Camerons or the Macdonalds, could not be extirpated ; there would be some bitter fighting, and then, when the lesson had been learned, there would be peace.

Yes, but what of the lesser septs ? The Appin Stewarts ? They would not be an easy folk to shepherd, for they had the sea and the sea islands for a refuge. The Glencoe men ? . . . He pulled himself up sharply, for he realised that Glencoe was precisely the kind of case he dreaded.

The clan there was a branch of the Macdonalds, but cut off in a long chasm of a glen from their kinsmen. They were a small people,

VIEW OF GLENCOE

Photo by G. P. Abraham Ltd.

less than a quarter of the clans of Maclean or
Sleat or Glengarry or Lochiel, less than half
of Appin or Keppoch. But they could muster
fifty fighting men in the field, and they were
natural warriors. They had been at Killiecrankie and afterwards with Buchan and
Cannon ; they were Catholics, and staunch
Jacobites, and ill regarded by Government.
They were cattle thieves like the rest, and un-
happily their raids took them into the domains
of potent and revengeful people like Argyll
and Breadalbane. Argyll hated them because,
like Appin, they formed a salient that jutted
into his own territory. Breadalbane had all
manner of ancient grudges against them, and
in the June conference at Achallader he had
had high words with their chief MacIan over
an alleged theft of cows, and had threatened
to do him a mischief—Hill had this direct
from the chief's son.

He had long known MacIan—as a young
man he had given Monk no trouble—and
had liked him for his high spirit and good
nature ; no Highlander was better spoken
of for fidelity to his word and courage in battle
than that gigantic old man. He had liked, too,

38

the second son, Alasdair, one of Buchan's captains, who for some time had been his prisoner at Inverlochy. He could not think happily of that little clan at the mercy of callous Lowland lawyers like Stair and ruthless intriguers like Breadalbane. Achtriachtan and Inverrigan had made their peace, but there was no word of any movement by the other MacIans. The fools, the pitiful fools, when the sword of Damocles hung above their heads !

Anxiety had driven out of Hill's mind his own grievances. This was a miserable business just when the Highlands were settling down. For months he had been writing to Livingstone and the Council that the whole district was peaceable and civil. Peaceable and civil— these had been his very words. Except for a little raiding in the Rough Bounds the land had been at ease. Yet in a month's time it might be in the throes of a bloody war. The best news he could get would be that every chief in Lochaber was posting to Inveraray or Inverness. Especially those stubborn fools of Glencoe, who were certain to be the first burnt-offering.

From his window he had a view of a corner of the barrack square, and the road from the main entrance. There seemed to be the stir of some arrival. In the gathering darkness he had a glimpse of a man dismounting from horseback. It could not be one of his patrols, for no patrols had gone out that day in the wild weather. It could not be his deputy Hamilton returning, for he was not expected back from the south yet awhile. He moved from the window as an orderly entered with a lamp, and behind him his major, Culloden's brother.

The latter's weather-beaten face was puckered in a grin. 'Who do you think is here, sir?' he asked. 'A penitent seeking mercy. No less than Glencoe himself!'

'Glencoe!' Hill cried. 'Bring him here instanter. The very man I have had in my mind all afternoon.'

Major Forbes ushered in a remarkable figure of a man. He was very tall, nearly six and a half feet, but so broadly made that his massiveness rather than his height was what first caught the eye. He had the dark wild eyes of Clan Donald, and a fierce nose like the beak of a galley. His white hair fell almost to his shoulders, and two great moustachios like buck's horns gave him the air of a Norse sea-king. His age was nearer seventy than sixty, but he held himself like a youth. In his bonnet was a bunch of faded heather, the Macdonald badge. He had trews of the dark tartan, and huge riding-boots of untanned leather, his broad belt carried a dirk and a brace of pistols, and at his side swung a long sword. He wore a fine buff coat, instead of the doublet of bull's hide for which he was famous. Hill knew the tale of that coat—it had been part of the plunder of Edinglassie, and had been often referred to in the processes of forfeiture against Dundee's followers. . . . He had not seen the man for thirty years. The Governor of Inverlochy reflected ruefully that age had dealt more kindly with this turbulent chieftain than with a docile servant of the law like himself.

The old man held up his right hand in salutation.

'It is MacIan,' he said. 'He has come to take the Government's oath.'

'You have been too long about it,' Hill replied drily, for his anxiety had made him

41

irritable. 'Why do you come here? You should be at Inveraray.'

'You are the Governor of Inverlochy.'

'I am a soldier, and the law ordains that the oath must be taken before a civil officer.' He picked up a paper from the table. 'These are the words of his Majesty's proclamation :— *" The persons who have been in arms before the time foresaid, and shall plead and take benefit of this our gracious indemnity, shall swear and sign the oath of allegiance to us by themselves, or the sheriff clerk subscribing for such as cannot write, and that before famous witnesses, betwixt and the first day of January next to come, in presence of the Lords of our Privy Council—or the sheriff—or their deputes— of the respective shires where any of the said persons live."* The words are explicit. Only a civil officer can swear you.'

Hill spoke tartly, for this was an old grievance of his. He had often urged that the Governor of Inverlochy should have the powers of a civil magistrate, as he had had in Monk's day.

'Three months back you received Achtriachtan,' the old man protested.

'I received Achtriachtan into the King's

peace, and gave him a written protection, but I warned him that he had not fulfilled the law, and must go to Inveraray to complete his submission. You knew that, MacIan, you and your clan. In May last you were willing to go to Argyll at Inveraray, you and your cousins of Appin.'

' That was in May,' was the answer. ' Since then I am not liking the name of Campbell. I was at Achallader in June and had ill words from the fox of Breadalbane.' He spoke good English, with the soft lilting accent of the Gael.

Hill laughed. ' I have been informed of that. My lord Breadalbane had somewhat against you in the matter of cattle-lifting.'

MacIan drew himself up.

' There was talk of that, but it was a lawful act of war. After the death of the Graham, Coll of Keppoch and we of Glencoe, returning to our homes, drove a booty from Glenlyon who was an enemy of our King. Was that a greater fault than the killing of the red soldiers at Killiecrankie, for which your Government offers pardon ? '

' That was not the first cause of offence given to my lord Breadalbane ? '

43

MacIan's gravity broke into a smile.

'Maybe no. Glencoe has never loved Glenorchy—or Glenlyon, since Mad Colin hung thirty-six braw men of ours on the Meggernie braes. Maybe it is true that cattle beasts from Glenorchy have sometimes found themselves in Coire Gabhail, and that there has been some dirking of Campbells by MacIans. Gentlefolk will always be bickering if they live too near, and be gartering their hose tighter when the nights grow dark. But the MacIans have never wronged their neighbours as Breadalbane has, or by a coward's law pleas and dirty parchments stripped them of the lands they heired from their fathers.'

'No. I never credited your clan with a taste for parchments. . . . But let us talk sense, for this is a grave business. You are within the danger of the law for your doings in the late rebellion. You have incurred the undying hatred of the most powerful folk in the Highlands, Argyll and Breadalbane. The King in his mercy offers you a way of peace. What do you do? First you come to the wrong place— to Inverlochy—to me, who can do nothing for you.'

44

JOHN CAMPBELL, 1st EARL OF BREADALBANE

*(From the portrait by Sir J. B. Medina in the Scottish National
Portrait Gallery)*

'I am a soldier, and would make my submission to a soldier.'

'A plague upon your punctilios. I tell you, though I were Schomberg or Talmash I would be powerless. The law says a civil officer. . . . Secondly, you put it off till the last moment. In two days it will be the New Year and the period of mercy will have closed. Was that not blind folly, with the menace of an offended Government hanging over you, and your good friends of Glenlyon and Glenorchy waiting for their revenge?'

The old man's face was troubled.

'I did only as others did. How many have sworn? Lochiel is but now gone to Inveraray.'

'So you know that? But Lochiel is in a different case from you. He is the head of a big clan, and Argyll has always been his friend. Glengarry has not sworn, but he has a strong castle and is ill to come at. You are a little people, and you have no friends near by, and the great folk love you as a shepherd loves a fox, and you are so situate that Glencoe can be inclosed like a nut between the crackers.'

The other's eyes grew more troubled, but his voice was proud.

'As one fighting man to another so I speak
to you, Colonel, and I will tell you the naked
truth. I could not take my oath to your
Government.' (Hill noticed that he said
'Government' and never 'King'—for him
there could be but the one king.) 'Not till I
was assured that a certain hope had gone.
You say truly that we of Glencoe are a small
people, but we have had no traitors among us
since the daughter of MacHenry first brought
the glen to Clan Donald. The men of Ian
Abrach draw their blood from Ian Og Fraoch,
the son of that Angus Og who sheltered King
Robert in his castle of Dunaverty in the south.
Our race and our religion make us true to the
lawful line of kings, and though we were to be
swept from the earth we could not forswear
that allegiance save by our King's order.'

'That order is come?'

'Such is the word brought to me.'

'Well, you are in the devil's own predica-
ment. Loyalty is a high virtue, MacIan,
though yours is a thought perverse. We were
friends in youth and I would fain help you. I
cannot receive you into the King's peace.
You must get you to Inveraray, and you have

47

two days to do it in. In this foul weather you may be hard put to it and be late for the fair. Have you any well-wishers there ? '

' I have many illwishers, and the chief of them is MacCailein Mor himself.'

' Argyll is not in the town at present, which is the better for you. Sir Colin Campbell is the sheriff-depute.'

' Ardkinglas, though a Campbell, is an honest man,' said the chief.

' I am happy to agree with you. He is also my friend, and I will write him a letter. Go straight to Ardkinglas and do not meddle with Duncanson the procurator-fiscal, for he has no good-will to any of your name.'

Hill sat down at the table and took up his pen, reading aloud each sentence as he wrote it. He begged Ardkinglas to receive this ' lost sheep ' who had misread his Majesty's proclamation and sought peace in the wrong quarter. Though MacIan were a day or two late—for the weather in Lochaber was severe— let a point be stretched and his submission be received. He subscribed himself his friend and well-wisher and colleague in the great task of peace-making.

48

As he sanded the ink he observed that MacIan had set his bonnet on his head and was rebuttoning his buff coat as if for instant departure. The chief took the letter, placed it in an inner pocket, and offered his hand. ' May God and the saints have you in keeping,' he said. ' In two hours I must be beyond Loch Leven.'

' Not so,' said Hill. ' Prayer and provender never yet hindered a man. You will sup with me—I have something better than the salted mart, for the last frigate brought certain Lowland delicacies—and you will sleep here. The wind is veering, and I think there will be no more snow.'

He was wrong. At three in the morning when, by the light of a waning moon, MacIan mounted his shelty and, attended by his four running footmen, turned his face down Loch Linnhe, the wind still set icily from the north-west, and the snow was again falling. Hill, who in a greatcoat and nightcap saw him off, watched the little party disappear in the brume. ' If he does not perish in a drift,' he muttered to himself, ' he will be a week late. God send that Ardkinglas be merciful ! '

D

CHAPTER II

INVERARAY AND EDINBURGH

MacIan and his gillies took the road down
Loch Linnhe in a thick downfall of snow. The
drifts were small, for the full force of the wind
was cut off by the Ardgour hills. It was still
black darkness when they reached the narrows
of Loch Leven, and found on the beach the
boat by which they had crossed the previous
afternoon. Here, too, there was some shelter
from the storm, and they made the passage
without difficulty. Three miles on the left a
light twinkled. That came from MacIan's
own house of Carnoch at the foot of Glencoe,
where his kin waited anxiously to hear the
result of his errand. One of the gillies was sent
off with a message, but he himself had no time
to waste. The quickest route to the south, had
it been summer-time, was up the Laroch
stream, between Ben Vair, the ' Mountain of
Lightnings,' and his own Meall Mor, and so

by Glen Creran to Connel Ferry, but in this weather a fox or a deer could not have made that journey. He turned to the right and took the shore road through Appin.

Dawn came upon them near Duror, a dawn of furious winds and solid driving snow. Happily it was a fine snow with sleet in it, and so it did not greatly clog the path, but the force of the gale was enough to lift a man off his feet. The running gillies, bent double, their bonnets dragged over their brows, their wet kilts plastered about their thighs, and their bare legs purple with the cold, felt it less than the chief on his shelty. He brought the folds of his plaid twice round his throat, but even so, and for all his years of hardihood, he felt numbed and crippled by the savagery of the heavens. Not a wild thing, bird or beast, was stirring— they knew better ; but he himself dare not seek shelter, though the warm chimney-corner of Ardsheal awaited him a mile off. For he knew that he was riding on a mission of life and death. He tried to comfort his heart by reminding himself that the great Montrose had travelled this very road at the same time of year before that fight at Inverlochy when he

set the heather above the gale. But Montrose
had had open weather for his march, and the
gale seemed now for good to have overtopped
the heather.[1]

They made slow progress, and midday found
them no further than Appin Kirk. At the inn
of Creagan they had a dram of hot whisky and
a bite of bread and cheese. But the wind there
was so fierce that the ferryman dare not trust
his coble on the water, and they were compelled to go round by the head of Loch Creran,
a circuit of several miles. MacIan's hope was
to be beyond Loch Etive before nightfall—
maybe even to reach the inn at Taynuilt under
Cruachan. But with the afternoon the wind
grew stronger and the snowfall more resolute,
and it was almost dark when he reached
Barcaldine, where the road turned south
through Benderloch to the sea.

Whether he had desired it or not he had to
halt at Barcaldine, for the road passed close
to the castle, and half a dozen fellows in the
Campbell tartan ran out to bar it. They
recognised the old man, and their faces were

---

[1] The heather is the Macdonald badge ; the gale, or bog-
myrtle, the Campbell.

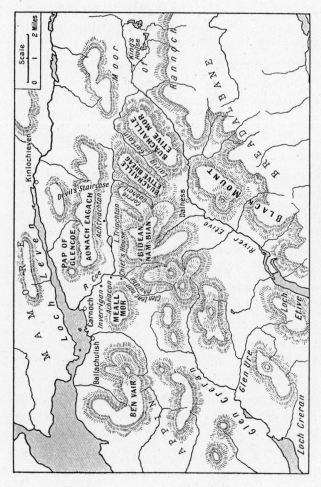

MAP OF GLENCOE AND NEIGHBOURHOOD

not kind. MacIan knew the place too well, the keep, built long ago by Duncan of the Seven Castles, which commanded the shore road from Appin to Lorn. He cursed the fate that had brought him within its pale, for the Campbells of Barcaldine were near kin to Breadalbane, and one of them had been the companion of that fox when he carried war into Caithness.

As he had feared, the garrison was of Glenorchy men. Its commander was a Captain Drummond, one of Breadalbane's Tayside neighbours, and the troops were of Argyll's regiment. MacIan presented Hill's letter, but at first Drummond would not read it. He had all the Lowland ill manners, so hateful to the Gael, who would use an enemy like a gentleman till he dirked him. The old man was treated half as spy and half as prisoner, given bare quarters and coarse food, and held under constant surveillance. He spent a night of anxiety and discomfort, but in the morning Drummond had relented. After all, he dare not offend Hill, for he and his men were under orders for the Inverlochy garrison. MacIan had something of a breakfast and was told that he might continue his journey, but it was not till the afternoon that his gillies were dug out from a noisome cellar, his shelty recovered, and a start made.

Twenty-four precious hours had been lost. Late that night the party reached Taynuilt, and as he got to bed MacIan heard a clock strike midnight. The New Year had begun and the time of probation was officially past.

Next day, in a second snowstorm, they struggled up the Pass of Brander beside a swollen river, and came to Loch Awe, scourged by a thousand blasts from the gullies of Cruachan. Never had he known such a blizzard. Five or six miles an hour were nothing to his long-limbed gillies, but now in an hour they could cover less than a mile. The snow was drifting too, and often they had to take to the rough hillside which the winds had swept bare. Darkness was on them before they had left the loch, and they spent the night in an empty sheiling. By the next morning, the second day of January, the storm had abated, and early that forenoon they dropped down Glen Aray to the little burgh which lay snug in the trench of its sea-loch.

Here MacIan had staggering news. He was two days late, and Ardkinglas, the sheriff-depute, was not there to receive him. Sir Colin had gone on a Hogmanay visit to kinsfolk, he was told, and had no doubt been storm-stayed.

For three wretched days the old man abode in Inveraray. Hill's letter was protection enough and had been received respectfully by the sheriff's office, but the burgh was not a healthy place for his tartan, and, with half the people still festive from the Hogmanay revels, there would be a certainty of brawls if it were seen in the streets. So he and his men found quarters in an obscure hostelry, and stayed indoors all day, while MacIan morning and evening visited the sheriff's house to get news of the laggard Sir Colin. He was miserably anxious, for he saw that his delay had given a supreme chance to his enemies. If the sheriff stood on the letter of the law, as he was entitled to do, his estates were forfeit and he and his clan were broken men—nameless, landless, like the wretched Macgregors. Ill-omened memories came to haunt him. A spaewife had prophesied that he would be murdered in his own house. He was resolved that that house should not see him again till he returned to it with the Government pardon in his pocket.

On the third day—the fifth of January—Sir Colin came back to town, rosy from his travels. He was a just man, whose patriotism was for all the Highlands and not merely for his clan, and he earnestly desired peace. He read Hill's letter and read it again, and knit his brows. For he was in a quandary. MacIan had missed his chance, and the law should take its course ; he had no power to extend the period laid down in the King's proclamation. But if he refused to receive him, MacIan's life would be forfeit, for he was aware of the hounds waiting to be unleashed, and he had an honest man's tenderness for one whom he knew to be an honest foe.

'What makes you so dooms behindhand?' he asked, and was told the storm and the detention at Barcaldine—not to mention the initial mistake of the bootless errand to Inverlochy.

'Well, you're in a fine creel. I see nothing for it but that I should decline to give you the oath. The thing's clean beyond my power.'

The old man, knowing that here was no enemy, but a perplexed friend, humbled his

57

pride and begged for mercy. He even wept,
he whose eyes were not used to tears. Let him
be permitted to take the oath, he said, and
every man of his clan would do the like ; if
any refused, he would be sent to prison or
impressed for the Flanders wars. Sir Colin
was moved, and finally persuaded.

' Come back the morn,' he said, ' and I'll
see what can be done for you.'

When MacIan returned on the 6th of
January, the sheriff-depute had made up his
mind. ' I'll swear you,' he said, ' but, mind,
I cannot guarantee that the thing is in order.
Our sheriff-clerk is in Edinburgh, and I will
send the certificate to him, and get him to take
the opinion of the Council on the matter. Not
that I think they will quarrel with what I have
done, for no more than me do they want
further dispeace in the Highlands. Likewise
I will write a letter to Colonel Hill, asking him
to give you and yours full interim protection.
That is the best I can do for you, MacIan,
but I think it will suffice. It is not likely that
the Council will question my judgment. You
can sleep sound in your bed in yon fearsome
black glen of yours.'

That afternoon in better weather the chief departed thankfully from the town of Inveraray, which seemed to his mountain eyes part miracle and part prison. He had no fear for his safety. The Campbell word was law now in the land, and in Argyll Sir Colin was the second greatest Campbell.

After his departure Ardkinglas, according to his promise, wrote to his namesake Colin Campbell, the sheriff-clerk of Argyll, now in Edinburgh, enclosing the certificate of Mac-Ian's submission and asking that it should be declared by the Council to be in order. He also wrote to the Governor of Inverlochy commending Glencoe to his protection, but for some reason omitted to send off the letter for three days. But one important missive he despatched at once by a special messenger. He sent an account of the whole business to his chief Argyll in London.

The further history of the certificate of Mac-Ian's oath is obscure. The Scottish Privy Council in that month of January was not greatly interested in the pacification of the clans ; to it, and to William, a more urgent

59

matter was the coming General Assembly of the Kirk and what might be the policy of the Presbyterian hot-heads. The certificate duly reached the hands of the sheriff-clerk in Edinburgh, who took it to the clerks of the Council, Sir Gilbert Elliot, the founder of the Minto family, and Mr. David Moncrieff. They naturally refused to receive it, since the time limit had expired. Thereupon the sheriff-clerk, along with Mr. John Campbell, a Writer to the Signet, took the opinion of a lord of Session, Lord Aberuchill, also a Campbell. There seems to have been no question of clan bias, for these Campbells may be presumed to have been anxious to do Ardkinglas's will. Aberuchill, who was a member of the Privy Council, put the matter before several of his colleagues, one of whom was the new Lord Stair, the father of Sir John Dalrymple. They gave it as their view that the certificate could not be accepted without a special warrant from the King, and accordingly it was scored through and cancelled.

The matter was never brought before the Council as a whole, though such had been Ardkinglas's intention, for there was no need

JOHN DALRYMPLE, 1st EARL OF STAIR

*(From the portrait by Sir J. B. Medina in the Scottish
National Portrait Gallery)*

of that if good legal opinion held that the Council had no power to extend the time. We need not suspect malign Dalrymple influence, for the decision was on the face of it sound law ; the Proclamation of August 27 permitted the oath to be taken before the Lords of the Council as well as before the sheriffs, but gave neither of these parties any power to vary its conditions.

It is more difficult to explain why the matter was not referred to London and the King's pleasure taken. The probable reason was that before this could be done—for the wheels of Scottish justice moved slow—word came that the fate of MacIan had already been decided. For the next stage of the drama we must turn to the South.

CHAPTER III

KENSINGTON

I

A CHIEF actor must now be introduced on the stage. The day is the 11th of January in the year 1692. The scene is the palace of Kensington, which William had bought from Lord Nottingham and made his chief dwelling, because he found Whitehall bad for his asthma and Hampton Court too remote from London.

A man sat in a warm wainscoted room with a table of papers before him. He congratulated himself that in this wintry weather his business with the King gave him quarters in the palace, so that he was not compelled to jog twice a day along the miry footpad-haunted roads which linked Kensington village with the capital. Now and then he cast a glance from the window at the new Dutch garden in which workmen were busy, and thought that he might well borrow a hint from it for his own Galloway home of Castle Kennedy. But chiefly he kept his eyes on his papers, for he had much troublesome business on hand.

The occupant of the chair was a handsome full-bodied man in his forty-fourth year. Sir John Dalrymple, now Master of Stair, was a figure not easily forgotten. The face framed in the huge perruque was immensely intelligent. The eyes under the broad brow were cool, wary and commanding. The lips were full but compressed, there was humour at the corners of the mouth, and the heavy jowl had a jovial, almost porcine, air. Yet the impression left upon the spectator was not that of geniality, but of a mocking competence, an almost arrogant self-complacency. And something more—something subtle and tortuous, a warning that this man would not be easily fathomed, and might be an uncertain colleague and a precarious friend. The seventeenth-century chroniclers were fond of finding ' *aliquid insigne* ' in their characters' faces—Sir Philip Warwick found it in the Duke of Hamilton's, and Clarendon in the younger Vane's. This something extraordinary was beyond doubt in the mobile countenance of the man in the chair.

He came of a strange family. His father, Sir James, the first Viscount Stair, had raised himself from a small Ayrshire lairdship to the peerage, the repute of the greatest Scots lawyer of the day, and a share in the inner councils of the King. He had been many things in his time—soldier, professor, advocate, lord of Session; he had quarrelled first with Lauderdale and then with Claverhouse; though no fanatic he had tried to protect the Covenanters, and had been for some years an exile in Holland before he returned with William. He had written on religion and on the law—on the latter so profoundly that he still ranks as the great institutional jurist of his country. His ability all men admitted, but few trusted him and fewer liked him. There was something uncanny about him and his race; he had a masterful wife whose piety did not save her from charges of dabbling in forbidden arts; fate seemed to brood over the house of Stair as it shadowed the house of Atreus, and a daughter and a grandson were the centre of tragic tales.

The son's life had been not less chequered than the father's. He had been more than once in prison, and had often gone in danger of his head. He had been Claverhouse's bitter enemy, yet he had become James's Lord Advocate, and had been responsible for the prosecution of James Renwick, the last martyr of the Covenant. He had taken the chief part in offering the crown of Scotland to William, and had had the difficult task of managing William's business in the first Scottish parliaments. Now, with the King often abroad at the wars, he was the virtual ruler of Scotland, for his colleague in the north, Johnston of Wariston, was a trivial being. He had as few friends as his father, and far more avowed enemies, since the Jacobites hated him as a turncoat, and the extreme Presbyterians as a trimmer and a Laodicean. He admitted the second charge, for if there was one thing he detested it was high-flying religion. As to the first, his defence was that he had served James only to prepare the way for the inevitable revolution, since he had always been William's man. He flattered himself that he had been a consistent Whig.

The man was not all of one piece. He had a human side known to his few intimates. In

66

private life he was notably good-natured, and his conversation was full-flavoured and merry. Sometimes in debate his dignity would break down, and he would scold an opponent like a fishwife. But the figure he presented in public affairs was clean-cut, impregnable, and highly unsympathetic, for alone of Scottish statesmen he had a policy, and the determination to enforce it. Let us try to set down the ideas at the back of his head.

He had his father's legal mind, but he was several stages further off than his father from the turbid old Scots world of fevered beliefs and unprofitable loyalties. He was emphatically the man of a new age, with something of the same outlook as Somers and Halifax. He sought order and reason and civilisation, and he hated all that he believed to stand in the way of these blessings. They were his faith, though he was sceptical about most things.

For a sentimental Jacobitism he had only scorn, and of religious fanaticism he was wholly intolerant. He honestly desired that Scotland should settle down into reputable ways, when her citizens should be secure in life and goods, and could advance from their present grinding

67

poverty to the prosperity which he believed to
be within their compass. He remembered too
bitterly what had happened before the Revolution to wish to see that anarchy perpetuated.

Also, for he was a statesman with a wide
vision, he saw the needle-point upon which
Britain stood. A little laxness here, a blunder
there, would shiver the brittle framework of
peace. Jacobitism was still a cave of Adullam
to which might resort the multitudinous forces
of discontent. Quiet at home was the first
essential, for William, of whom he was the
loyal servant, was fighting a desperate battle—
how desperate was only known to a man like
him who had lived with the King in his
Flanders camps. He was opposing with weak
allies the greatest monarch and the most for-
midable confederation in the world. He had
to face Luxemburg, the little, harsh-featured
hunchback who was the foremost military
genius of the day, the greatest general pro-
duced by the house of Montmorency ; a
brilliant second in Boufflers ; and a sagacious
war minister in Louvois. Ireland was for the
moment quiescent, but the continental campaign of 1691 had been a failure, with the loss

WILLIAM III

(From the portrait by Jan Wyck in the National Portrait Gallery

of Mons and the defeat at Leuse, and the omens were not bright for the new year. It was his business to see that no folly at home crippled the force of the British stroke beyond the Channel.

The Master of Stair was a Lowlander with most of the merits and every defect of that stalwart breed. The virtues which he respected were order, sobriety, prudence, industry ; he had no taste for the romantic glories and little patience with them. His blood was cool and his imagination strictly disciplined. Not only was he a Lowlander, but he was a son of that south-west region of Scotland where the Lowland qualities of individualism and independence were found in their most truculent form. Small as his liking had been for the Covenant, he had tried to protect the Covenanters, realising that, though in a temporally perverted form, they had the virtues which might make the kind of citizens he desired to see. Therefore he was utterly impatient with those who preferred a romantic whimsy to common sense, and with all the sentimental rodomontade for which his old enemy Claverhouse had died. If Scotland was

ever to become a civilised land it must get rid
of this lumber of the Middle Ages.

Above all he was intolerant of the Highlands.
It shocked his orderly mind that one half of
Scotland should be as barbarous as the wilds of
America. He had to the full the Lowland
hatred and fear of those northern mists from
which time and again had come banditti to
trouble the peace of Scotland. The Highlands
were the home of a clan system which was half
autocratic and half communal, and in both
respects hateful to a Whig. They were the last
refuge of Jacobitism. The life was barbarous
and brutal, and the King's writ ran limpingly.
There lay the danger-point, and if the peril
was to be crushed it must be done at once, for
the present police force, Leven's and Argyll's
regiments, would soon be required in Flanders.
He had never crossed the Highland line, but
he had met Highlanders, and he liked them
little—Glengarry, Lochiel, Appin and the rest
of them, huge, flamboyant, witless bravos.

Fortunately there were some few Highlanders
who were on the side of common sense. Tarbat
was one ; he had no great love for Tarbat, but
at any rate he talked the language of educated

men and he knew on which side his bread was
buttered. Argyll, too ; a trumpery creature,
but his interests were now solid for the Government. Breadalbane—and at the thought of
Breadalbane the Master lay back in his chair
and pondered. This was the hardest nut of all
to crack, and the most important in the platter.

The man was in town. He had come up at
Christmas to report. He had been at the
palace that very morning. Breadalbane's face
rose before Dalrymple, for in his sleeping and
waking hours it was a constant enigma to him ;
and well it might be, for the face as it looks at
us from the canvas of Sir John Medina seems
to have been formed to conceal the soul behind
it. It has the gravity of a Roman senator and
the proud stateliness of a Spanish hidalgo ; the
mouth is steadfast and not unkindly, the eyes
under the heavy lids have a sober dignity.
Dalrymple flattered himself that he had no
illusions about Breadalbane. He knew his
past in all its shamelessness, a past of money-
lending, blackmail, oppression, chicanery, and,
when the need arose, of violence and murder.
He knew that to the core he was avaricious
and selfish, with no higher thought than his

money-bags and his rent-rolls. He was aware
that he had been deep in many treasons, and
even now was suspected on good evidence of
having intrigued in the summer on James's
behalf with the Highland chiefs. He knew that
he was the most comprehensively distrusted
man in all Scotland.

But there was much to be said on the other
side. No one denied his remarkable abilities.
After Argyll he could bring more men into
the field than any Highland grandee. And,
like Dalrymple, he wanted peace. It stood to
reason that he did, for his great domains, which
stretched from Loch Awe to the haughs of Tay,
were especially at the mercy of disorder.
Behind him were the savage clans of Lochaber
who loathed the name of Campbell, and had
a readier access to his lands than they had to
Argyll's. A settlement of the Highlands would
enable him to reap in comfort what he had
sown through fifty disreputable years. William
could offer him more than James, for if the
Stuarts returned it would be Glengarry and
Sleat and Clanranald who would be in favour,
not Breadalbane, however much he might have
contributed to that return.

Besides, he had a policy. Breadalbane knew his countrymen and had no doubt about the proper course. He had done his best with the scheme of bribing the clans, but that had failed. He had not opposed the King's proclamation of August. But he had been very clear about what the next step should be, if submission did not follow. The next proclamation must be written with a sharp pen and bloody ink. ' Mauling' was his phrase : the recalcitrants must be so handsomely mauled that their will to resist would be crushed for ever. All the rebels, if possible, but if not, a selected few like Keppoch and Glencoe as an example. He had argued his case brilliantly, and Dalrymple had been convinced, for this man knew the nature of the Gael.

Yet as he lay back in his chair he was not quite at ease on the point. After all, the man had been one of the leaders of the Highland host which ten years ago had descended upon his own westlands. It was odd company for a Whig to find himself in. He had staked a good deal on Breadalbane and his nicely calculated honesty. He had written him letters which might some day be brought up against him.

That day a Highland policy must be deter-
mined on, and he was still in two minds.
There was a long *dossier* on the subject, and he
must refresh his memory about the past. From
a drawer in the table he took a bundle of
papers, for he was a careful man and made his
secretary copy every letter of importance to
which he put his name.

II

Eight months ago he had been sanguine that
the King's law could be brought to the Highlands without further bloodshed. He hated
war—it was not his business, and he did not
understand it, and he most earnestly desired
a peaceful settlement. He had flung himself
heart and soul into Tarbat's scheme of bribing
the chiefs, and, because Breadalbane seemed
the best agent, he had laid himself out to con-
ciliate Breadalbane. How many letters had he
not indited to him last summer from those com-
fortless Flanders camps ! On June 25th he had
written to encourage him in his negotiations.
' If they will be mad, before Lammas they will
repent it, for the army will be allowed to go

into the Highlands, which some thirst so much for, and the frigates will attack them ; but I have so much confidence of your character and capacity to let them see the ground they stand on, that I think these suppositions are vain.' A month later he had begged Breadalbane to get the clans to meet him in Edinburgh, and in the meantime he had been warning Livingstone that no acts of hostility should be committed against the Highlanders.

On September 28 from Loo he had encouraged Breadalbane to persevere in the good work, and urged that nothing should be done to exacerbate Highland feeling by undue suspicion. ' The best cure of all these matters is, that the chieftains do it (take the oath) as quickly as can be, which will take off the trials or suspicions against the rest.' Two days later he told him that he had spoken to the King about the money required, which would be forthcoming when needed, and reiterated his belief in his honesty, which so many were doubting. ' The best evidence of sincerity,' he had written, ' is the bringing the matter quickly to a conclusion. . . . I hope your lordship shall not only keep them (the clans) from giving any offence,

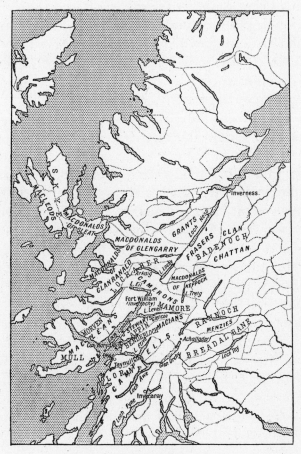

MAP OF THE WESTERN CLANS

but bring them to take the allegiance which they ought to do very cheerfully, for their lives and fortunes they have from their Majesties.'

The Master raised his head and considered. His conscience was clear. Never had man been more earnest in the cause of peace.

He turned the pages of the file and was reminded how in early December his hopes had begun to wane. There was a brief letter to Hamilton, Hill's second-in-command at Inverlochy, warning him that the garrison might soon have to take the field on a punitive expedition, 'for the winter-time is the only season in which we are sure the Highlanders cannot escape us, nor carry their wives, bairns and cattle to the mountains.' The bribery plan had failed, and the clans showed no signs of obeying the King's proclamation of August. He was back in London then, and closer in touch with home affairs, and it looked as if nothing remained but a winter expedition. There must be no delaying after the day of grace, January 1, was past, for the regiments of Leven and Argyll would soon be due for Flanders.

To Breadalbane he wrote on December 2

that he thought that Clan Donald should be rooted out, and his 'doited cousin' Lochiel. As for the rumours about Breadalbane's own conduct, he had discussed them with the King, who treated them as trifles. . . . He had not quite given up hope, for next day he wrote again to Breadalbane with the news that Tarbat had had letters from Glengarry, and had seen William, who had gone carefully into the proposed payments to the different chiefs. 'By the next I expect to hear either that these people are come to your hand, or else your scheme for mauling them, for it will not delay . . . I am not changed as to the expediency of doing things by the easiest means and at leisure, but the madness of these people and their ungratefulness to you makes me plainly see that there is no reckoning on them, but *delenda est Carthago*. Yet who have accepted, and do take the oath, will be safe, but deserve no kindness. . . . Therefore look on and you shall be satisfied of your revenge.'

The Master re-read the last letter, and with it another of the same date to Hamilton at Inverlochy. To the latter he had written : ' Let me hear from you with the first whether you think that this is the proper season to maul them in the cold long nights, and what force will be necessary,' and he added that he had written to the same purpose to Colonel Hill. Since the clans were apparently not coming in, it was very necessary to strike hard as soon as the new year began. Argyll's regiment was at Inverlochy, Leven's was at Inverness, and Buchan's (John the rubicund Whig, not his brother Thomas the sallow, saturnine Jacobite) was under notice to join it. What was in his mind was a brief vigorous campaign of mauling —'letters of fire and sword' in the old Scots phrase—the burning of hovels and stores, the driving away of cattle, and, when they resisted, the slaughter of men. It would be directed chiefly against Glengarry and his Macdonalds—'That's the only popish clan in the kingdom, and it will be popular to take severe courses with them.' This had always been Breadalbane's advice, and Breadalbane knew his countrymen.

There came a gap in the correspondence during the Christmas and New Year season, since Tarbat and Argyll and Breadalbane were all in London. For the first week of January

1692 the old plan stood. Here was his letter of the 7th to Livingstone, the Scottish commander-in-chief, informing him that the orders would go out next day. It should be a short and sharp business. These were his words : ' You know in general that those troops posted at Inverness and Inverlochy will be ordered to take in the house of Invergarry, and to destroy entirely the county of Lochaber, Lochiel's lands, Keppoch's, Glengarry's, Appin and Glencoe. If there be any opposition the troops (that is Leven's and Buchan's regiments) will need to join ; if not, they may act separately, which will make the work the shorter. I assure you their power shall be full enough, and I hope the soldiers will not trouble the Government with prisoners. The slighting the offered mercy, and depending still upon foreign assistance, will justify all the severity which can be used against those who can neither be obliged nor trusted. . . . It's true, it's a rigid season for the soldiers to work, but it's the only time they cannot escape you, for human constitutions cannot endure to be now long out of houses. A few days will do all that's at present either necessary or possible.'

The Master with his quill underlined these sentences. They seemed to him sound common sense. He was a convert to Breadalbane's view, the need of blood and iron. But in moderation. He had always prided himself upon being a moderate and humane man. A sharp lesson, after ample warning, would save much suffering in the future, and might bring to reason the chiefs who were now gambling with the lives of their wretched peoples. His policy was not extirpation—you could not extirpate the Macdonalds and the Camerons in a few days—but punishment.

A good policy, but now, alas! impossible. For the very next day had come news that the clans, after procrastinating to the last moment, had taken the oath. Lochiel and Appin had sworn at Inveraray—Glencoe too, so Hill reported ; and Keppoch at Inverness ; only Glengarry stood out. The whole plan of the punitive campaign had miscarried ; all that remained was to deal with Glengarry and his fortified castle, and a troublesome little expedition like that would have no solemnising effect upon the Highland mind. On the 9th he wrote to Livingstone : ' For my part I could have

wished the Macdonalds had not divided, and I
am sorry that Keppoch and MacIan of Glencoe
are safe. . . . I would be as tender of blood or
severities as any man, if I did not see the
reputation of the Government in question upon
slighted mercy, and the security of the nation
in danger by those who have been obstinate
to that degree that, if we believe them rational,
we must think they depend upon such assur-
ances of help that we can never oblige them
even to their own advantages from this
Government, and therefore it must make sure
of them.'

The Master restored the bundle of papers
to its drawer, and turned to the letter he had
begun to write. He had seen the King and
was sending his instructions to Livingstone
about the expedition against the few recalcitrants. The Macleans in Mull, about whom
there was some doubt, would be left to Argyll.
Sleat, who was also doubtful, was to be dealt
with. Glengarry, about whom there was no
doubt, was to be attacked and Invergarry taken.
William's inclinations were mild. Rebel chiefs
were to be given quarter, and the commonalty,

if they took the oath, were to be assured in
their lives and property. In the covering letter
to Livingstone the Master was emphasising this
mercifulness. 'I am most concerned,' he
wrote, 'for the poor commonalty. I do well
know, if nothing be done to disable them, they
will join with their lairds and chieftains when-
ever these appear. . . . I think they should have
some ease and feel the advantage of having the
King their master . . .'

He broke off to reflect upon his deep dis-
satisfaction with the whole business. There had
been a general taking of the oath, but it had
been insolently and defiantly put off till the
eleventh hour. Glengarry might be punished,
but that gave no security for peace, since
nothing would have been done to change the
Highland mind, no swift dramatic judgment,
such as Breadalbane had always pled for, which
would awe those barbarous but impressionable
souls. . . .

A servant announced that the Earl of Argyll
desired to see him. Argyll might throw more
light upon the business. The Master had no
belief in Argyll, either in his brains or in his

ARCHIBALD CAMPBELL, 1st DUKE OF ARGYLL

(*From the engraving after Sir J. B. Medina*)

character ; his prominent shifting eyes were an advertisement of his instability to all the world. But Argyll had means of getting news which never entered the official flying packets.

He resumed his letter to Livingstone with a fateful sentence. 'Just now my lord Argyll tells me that Glencoe hath not taken the oath, at which I rejoice. It's a good work of charity to be exact in rooting out that damnable sept—the worst in all the Highlands.' Ardkinglas's despatch to his chief had brought the news that, though MacIan had sworn, it had been six days too late. He was still within the law's danger.

III

During the next few days there were many consultations between the Master, Argyll and Breadalbane, and several interviews with the King. On the 16th William signed additional instructions to Livingstone, which concluded thus : ' If McKean of Glencoe, and that tribe, can be well separated from the rest, it will be a proper vindication of the public justice to extirpate that sept of thieves.'

That day the Master wrote to Livingstone telling him that the King would only receive recalcitrants now ' on mercy,' a reference to Glengarry; but 'for a just example of vengeance I entreat this thieving tribe in Glencoe to be rooted out in earnest.' To Hill he wrote on the same day in the same terms, but with an ominous addition. ' The Earls of Argyll and Breadalbane have promised they shall have no retreat in their bounds. The passes to Rannoch would be secured, and the hazard certified to the laird of Weem to retreat them. In that case Argyll's detachment, with a party that may be posted in Island Stalker, must cut them off.' On the 30th he told Livingstone : ' I am glad that Glencoe did not come in within the time prescribed. I hope what's done may be in earnest, since the rest are not in a condition to draw together to help. I think to herry their cattle or burn their houses is but to render them desperate, lawless men, to rob their neighbours ; but I believe you will be satisfied it were a great advantage to the nation that thieving tribes were rooted out and cut off. It must be quietly done, otherwise they will make shift for both the men and their cattle.'

To Hill, also on the 30th, he wrote : ' When anything concerning Glencoe is resolved, let it be secret and sudden.' And on the 23rd Livingstone had written to Hamilton telling him that he and the Inverlochy garrison would be judged according to how they handled Glencoe. The Court, he added, rejoiced that MacIan had not taken the oath in time, ' so that the thieving nest might be entirely rooted out.'

Argyll's news had given the Master a new policy. He now saw a chance for a dramatic stroke which would carry terror to every rebellious heart. In Scotland commissions of fire and sword had been frequent shot for the rusty blunderbuss of criminal justice, and as a learned lawyer he knew all about them. To ' destroy by fire and sword ' was the common style of proclamation against ' intercommuned rebels.' That treatment had long ago been meted out to the Macgregor clan. In 1640 Argyll, the famous Marquis, had been given such a commission against the Atholl and Ogilvy lands. The words had a specific meaning, and to ' extirpate ' did not mean to exterminate, but at the worst only to make a clan landless and chiefless. The attack was usually made by day and in summer, and involved burning of crops and houses and driving of cattle, but as a rule little loss of life. This was how the Master intended the Macleans to be handled by Argyll, and Glengarry by the Inverlochy and Inverness garrisons.

But as regards the MacIans he meant extermination. He wanted a spectacular punishment, and this seemed a chance for it. It would need an army to exterminate great clans like Glengarry's and Lochiel's, dwelling over a wide stretch of country ; even Keppoch, with open boundaries, would be hard to manage. But the MacIans in their ravine of Glencoe were a simpler matter. If the passes at either end were netted not a soul need escape.

How came this savage notion to dominate the mind of a politic and not inhumane statesman? The answer must be that he got it from Breadalbane and Argyll—but principally from Breadalbane. He wanted an exemplary sacrifice, and Breadalbane showed him where to find it. The Master himself knew less about Glencoe than he knew about the passes of the

Alps. He disliked the clan because he had
been told that they had been among the chief
obstacles to the bribing policy of the previous
summer, and that they were bitter Jacobites
and notorious caterans even beyond the aver-
age Highlander. Breadalbane told him these
things. He also pointed out that the physical
nature of Glencoe made the place a trap which
could be set and watched by a handful of
troops. No need to trouble about Leven's
and Buchan's regiments. He painted the
MacIans as a blot upon the Highlands, a mere
rabble of vermin, a disconsidered sept of Clan
Donald whom even the other Jacobite clans
would not study to avenge. His hatred and
his local knowledge made his arguments
weighty, and when he showed how he and
Argyll could block the bolt-holes the Master
was convinced. If we need further evidence
for Breadalbane's part, we may note the fact
that the executants of the tragedy were mostly
his creatures, and that an evil conscience
brought his steward to Glencoe after the
massacre to try to buy the silence of the
survivors.

The Master has come down to history with

a heavy weight of blood-guilt upon him, and, even if Breadalbane's crime was the more heinous, it is hard to say that his condemnation is undeserved. He chose to depart from the standards of the civilisation which he preached, partly because he allowed a consideration of policy to over-ride the human decencies, partly because he regarded the Highlands, and especially the MacIans, as something less than human. It should be observed that barbarous cruelty, the slaying of young and old, man and woman and child, is not the only charge, for the scheme involved treachery, though he may have had no inkling of the deeps to which that treachery was to descend. A man of his intelligence cannot have been ignorant that treachery was inevitable if his instructions were carried out to do the thing 'quietly' and to be 'secret and sudden.' He knew that the MacIans were living in fancied security, believing that Ardkinglas's acceptance of their oath had satisfied the law. Any sudden assault would be upon trusting and unsuspecting men. Having willed the end, he had willed also the unholy means.

How shall we apportion William's share?
I find it impossible to believe that he was not
a consenting party to the plan of wholesale
murder. He knew nothing of the Scots prac-
tice of 'fire and sword,' and the mild inter-
pretation given to the word 'extirpate'; to
him it must have borne its literal meaning.
The main instructions he countersigned at
the top as well as at the bottom, as if to
give them special authority, which weakens
Burnet's plea that he signed the document
without reading it.

It is clear from the correspondence that he
went meticulously into the business of the
payments to the chiefs, and that the Master
of Stair communicated to him every step he
took. He heard that MacIan had taken the
oath, though late; he knew that Glengarry,
who had not sworn at all, was to be merci-
fully treated; but he approved of the extermination of the little clan of Glencoe as a
politic expedient.

The fact that he did not punish the principal
malefactors when the truth became known is
another proof that he felt that he was deeply
implicated, for he was a man who was always

honest with himself. Technically he carried
the chief responsibility, for the measure was a
military act, and Hamilton and Livingstone
were not responsible to the Secretary for Scotland but to the King.

There is much to be said in extenuation.
He knew nothing of the Highlands, and regarded Glencoe as a mere robbers' den. He
was engaged in a life-and-death struggle, and
had small leisure to inform himself about what
he considered the uncouth barbarians of the
north. He had no love for Scotland, and
respected no Scotsmen but Carstares and the
Dalrymples, and he may well have thought
the blotting out of a few hundreds of its people
to be no very serious matter. He was a great
man, but neither humane nor gracious.

The burden of the scheme framed at Kensington in the latter half of January must rest
upon three men, Breadalbane, the Master, and
the King. The first has the heaviest share, the
last the lightest. The guilt varies with the
degree of knowledge, and the intimacy of the
relationship between the wronged and the
wronger. In William it was a crime against
humanity in general, in the Master of Stair

against his fellow Scots, and in Breadalbane against those who shared with him the blood and traditions of the Gael.

CHAPTER IV

GLENCOE

GLENCOE is a gash like a sword-cut among the loftiest and wildest of the Highland hills. At the western end of the Moor of Rannoch stand the sentinel Shepherds of Etive, and from their corries streams combine to form the infant Etive, which flows south-west to the sea-loch of that name, with on its left bank the *massif* of the Black Mount. North of the Shepherds the waters drain westward, and presently descend into a deep-cut glen, which stretches to Loch Leven. The northern wall is the long ridge of Aonach Eagach, the ' Notched Hill ' ; its south the two Shepherds, the Buachaille Etive Mor and the Buachaille Etive Bheag ; and then, going westward, the great bulk of Bidean nam Bian, the highest mountain in Argyll, till the ridge bends northward and sinks to the sea at Meall Mor.

The natural outlets are at the west, or sea

95

end, towards Ballachulish, and in the east to the inn of Kingshouse, whence the traveller can make his way to Rannoch and Lochaber, or south to Glenorchy and the Breadalbane country. In the nine miles of its length the glen has few entries on its flanks. There is no gap in the northern wall of Aonach Eagach save the old military road, which climbs by the Devil's Staircase towards Kinlochleven and Mamore. On the south side, beginning from the east, there is the pass called the Lairig Gartain, leading between the two Shepherds to Glen Etive. After that there are only chimneys for the cragsman, till, on the north-west side of Bidean nam Bian, the two glens of Fionn and Bhuidhe provide difficult routes to Glen Etive and Glen Creran. In all the Highlands there is no other such well-defended sanctuary.

Down in the valley bottom the river Coe, after leaving the bleak moorlands of its birth, runs in deep linns between buttresses of crag, till, midway in its course, it expands into the shallow and boggy Loch Triachtan. On the shelf north of the loch stood at that time the village of Achtriachtan, with the house of one of the cadet gentry of the clan. Thence it flows through natural woodlands, receiving on its left its main tributary from the corries of Bidean nam Bian. Just north of the point of junction stood another village, Achnacon, and a little further down the hamlet and farm of Inverrigan. The sea is now in sight, and among dunes and woodlands, some natural and some planted, stood the house of Carnoch, the principal house in the glen and the residence of the chief. The clan, apart from outlying shepherds' bothies and the high sheilings of the summer-time, lived around Carnoch, and in the three clachans of Achtriachtan, Inverrigan and Achnacon.

The marvels of the glen have been the theme of much prose and verse. Looking down it from the east in wild weather it can appear like some prison-house of the *Inferno*, but from the same standpoint, when the sun is sinking beyond Ardgour and the peaks are rose and gold above its purple abyss, it may seem a gateway to happy enchantments. The quartzite and schist formation, seamed by broad belts of porphyry, has contorted the rocks into fantastic shapes, which are grim or fairy-like

G   97

according to the light and the weather. I know no landscape so capricious in its moods. I have sat on a crag of Aonach Dubh and peered down through driving snow into what seemed to be a hyperborean hell ; and I have looked up the glen on a June evening, when the hills drowsed in a haze like sloeberry bloom and the clear streams crooned among flowers and grasses, so that the place seemed, in Neil Munro's words, one of the ' blessed corries, so endowed since the days when the gods dwelt in them without tartan or spear, in the years of peace that had no beginning.'

The savagery was only in the hills, for Glencoe itself was a fruitful and habitable place. There were juicy pastures by the stream and on the shelves of the two Shepherds, where black cattle could feed, and sheep and goats, and the ewe-milkers were busy on the summer mornings. It was sheltered from the north and east winds, and its winters were mild. Loch Leven and Loch Linnhe gave its people herrings and salmon, and the Coe was famous for its sea-trout. Oats and bear did well in the lower haughs. The hills were the haunt of the red deer, and the hazel coverts of roebuck, and

the ancient royal Forest of Dalness was part of
MacIan's territory and tenanted by a clans-
man. It is clear that Glencoe had a name not
for bleakness but for snugness and comfort.
' This countrie is verie profitable, fertill,' wrote
the seventeenth-century topographer, ' plen-
teous of corne, milk, butter, cheese and
abundance of fish.' ' A beautiful valley,'
wrote the author of the *Memoirs of Locheill*, and
the eighteenth-century report was ' a glen so
narrow, so warm, so fertile . . . a place of
great plenty and security.' It was a ' garden
enclosed ' as contrasted with the stony uplands
of Knoydart or Mamore.

The life of the little clan that dwelt there
was not the idyllic thing which some enthusiasts would have us picture it, but no more
was it the naked barbarism of current Lowland belief. The MacIans had their own type
of civilisation, their own economy, religion and
laws. They were of the old faith, though it is
not likely that a priest came often to celebrate
mass in Glencoe. They were reported among
their neighbours to be ' very resolute, hardy,
and stout, and to have the least vanity of any
of the septs of Clan Donald.' The society was

patriarchal, the chief being the protector of his people, and also the judge, in which duty he had behind him a great mass of ancient traditional law. No fault was ever found with MacIan on these scores. Their economy was rudimentary but by no means barbarous. They grew their own corn, which sufficed except in a season of dearth. In summer and autumn hunting gave them ample store of game and fish. For the winter cattle were salted down, and salmon kippered. The herring gabbarts from the Clyde brought them Lowland manufactured goods to be exchanged for their fish and skins. The surplus of the black cattle was sent south in droves to the Lowland fairs. A certain amount of money circulated, and luxuries were not unknown ; there was a smattering of education, and many could talk English and a little French.

Normally their life was peaceful, but now and then the crops would fail, the cattle could get no winter fodder, and after the ancient fashion the young men would go out to drive a prey from the lands of ancestral enemies. Behind all these raids, whether in Argyll or Breadalbane or further afield, there was always,

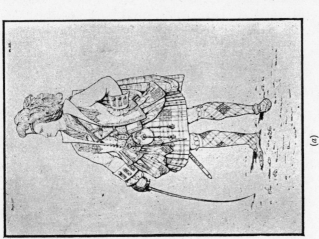

(b)

(a)

CONTEMPORARY HIGHLAND DRESS, I

it should be remembered, a sense of getting back that of which they had been unlawfully deprived. Sometimes, too, there was a matter of personal revenge, reprisals when there was no hope of otherwise obtaining justice. It has been truly said that the inefficiency of the Government was largely to blame for the law-lessness of the Highlands. In those raids and vendettas there was much blood and cruelty. Life for such folk was a hard thing ; they could suffer much, and were not chary of making others suffer ; but even the brutality was governed by iron rules which were never infringed. There were laws not to be broken —the sanctity of an oath, the inviolability of a guest. Their life was like that of the Homeric heroes, cruel and brutish, but controlled by certain taboos which were adamantine.

In actual comfort the society of the glen probably far exceeded that of a Lowland parish of the time. There was not the back-breaking monotonous toil on sour, ill-drained land. The chase gave their men healthy exer-cise. Their food was better, except in the depth of winter—full meals of flesh as con-trasted with the Lowland sowens and bear-

meal bannocks. Their bodies were better
nourished and developed. If they had no
Kirk to enforce discipline, they had a high-
handed chief. The houses were no worse, and
fuel was more plentiful. Occupations were
more varied, there was more social freedom,
and more light and colour in their lives. They
were worse citizens of Scotland, and of the
world, than the peasants of Penpont or Muir-
kirk, but in their own enclave they had a
richer and more wholesome civic life.

The keynote of such a society was a sense of
ancient civilisation and a pride of race, in
which every member of the clan shared. The
long past of Clan Donald was an intimate thing
to the humblest, almost like a living memory.
They could not forget that the sons of Ian
Abrach descended straight from that Angus
Og of Islay who was also the father of the
first Lord of the Isles. Tales ran in their heads
of which their own kin had been the heroes,
for there was no saga of the Isles in which they
could not claim a part. And not Clan Donald
alone, but their own little people had made a
name for valour that rang through the Highlands. Ninety years back had not certain

Moray lairds brought Alasdair MacIan Og of Glencoe to Morayland on a bond of maintenance to fight in their quarrels? A Glencoe man had guided Montrose in his famous descent upon Argyll.

The life in the glen, too, had its refinements and its hours of merriment. On the summer evenings on the haughs there would be tossing the cabar, and races among the young men, and fierce games of shinty. Up in the sheiling-huts in the twilight the girls would spin, or dance to the pipes, or listen to old tales and harpers' tunes. In the winter nights, when the birch billets made the peat fires leap, and the doors were shut, there would be snug gatherings; the old men at their tobacco, the wives at the spinning-wheel, and the young folk at their songs and tales. For great verse had been left to this little clan. Then would be heard the high deeds of Finn and Oscar, Caolte and Oisin, and the tragical tale of Deirdre, and a motley of adventures that made the breath catch and the blood run quick. Some of the stories came very near to them, for not twenty miles away to Loch Etive side had come the Sons of Uisnach.

Some of the songs, too, were their own. It was in the dark slit of Coire Gabhail that the fairies had whispered to the herd-girl the tune of *Crodh Chailein*, ' Colin's Cattle,' the most effective of all milking songs, and the sweetest of lullabies.

By the 8th of January MacIan was back in Glencoe, somewhat weary, but with a mind at peace. He summoned at once Achtriach-tan and the tacksman of Inverrigan.

' You have letters of protection from the Governor of Inverlochy,' he said, ' but they are not enough. You and all the males of my people must journey to Inveraray to take the oath, once the roads are open. Meantime I have sworn on your behalf, to see that Glencoe keeps the Government's peace. I have had kindness from Colin of Ardkinglas, and it must be repaid in strict honour. My children must bide as quiet in this glen as a hedgehog in its winter's hole. I, MacIan, have sworn it.'

He asked for news, and was told that word had come by way of Mamore that Glengarry and his clan were up, and that some of Argyll's men, under Robert of Glenlyon, had gone out against them. He frowned at the name.

105

' Robert of Glenlyon is a bad person to be
loose in Lochaber. Does son Alasdair know
that his bonny kinsman is so near ? It was
an ill day for Appin when he took auld Glenlyon's widow to wife.'

For the rest of January there were snow-
storms which levelled the clefts with the braes ;
frosts, too, which made every waterfall a stack
of silver spears. But that was on the high
hills ; in the valley bottom the fall soon melted.
Now and then came soft mild days when the
pastures showed bleached and sodden, and
Loch Triachtan was blue with the reflection
of the skies—the weather when, according to
the Gaelic saying, the badger turns in his
winter sleep and dreams of spring. The people
of the glen, who had had anxious minds at the
New Year, turned again to their several avoca-
tions. The women made the dyes of lichen
and heather and seaweed for the wool they
had spun, or wove that wool into plaiding ;
the old men mended cobles and steadings ;
and the young men were on the hill all day,
bringing back fat hinds, and now and then a
ptarmigan, or ranging .the woods for roebuck

and capercailzie, or on the shores of Loch
Triachtan at sunset when the wild duck
gathered.

Meantime, as we have seen, there was much
afoot in London, and the posts to the north
carried fateful letters. Livingstone, the commander-in-chief, received the King's instructions, dated January 16, and a covering letter
from the Master of Stair. The Master on the
same date wrote to Hill at Inverlochy, giving
the details of the plan as arranged with
Breadalbane—Argyll and Breadalbane watching the southern passes, the laird of Weem
cutting off all retreat into Perthshire (with
a special eye to the friendly Atholl clans),
and a detachment from Hill's garrison block-
ing escape towards the Moor of Rannoch.
Forbes, Hill's major, picked up this letter in
Edinburgh, and, according to his instructions
from his superior, broke the seals and for-
warded it to Inverlochy. On his journey
thither at the end of the month—he travelled
by Lorn and Appin—he fell in with some of
Argyll's regiment at the ferry of Ballachulish,
and learned that they were bound for quarters
in Glencoe.

When he reached Inverlochy he found Hill in a sad state. He had received the King's instructions and the Master's letter, and disliked the whole business. After getting the message from Ardkinglas he had given orders that the MacIans should be considered loyal subjects and in no way molested, and now here was a plan in train to root them out, a very different treatment to that proposed for the still rebellious Glengarry. That was bad enough, bad, he thought, as public policy, besides being a rebuff to himself. But what perturbed him more was Forbes's account of what he had seen at Ballachulish. Soldiers of the Argyll regiment, but all Breadalbane's men, and seeking lodging in Glencoe ! It looked as if some hideous piece of foul play were being meditated. He had virtually been superseded, too, for Livingstone was sending instructions direct to Hamilton, his second-in-command, and it was Hamilton who was managing the affair without confiding to him the details. His humanity and professional dignity were alike outraged.

But what could he do ? He could send in his papers. That would not stop the mischief,

108

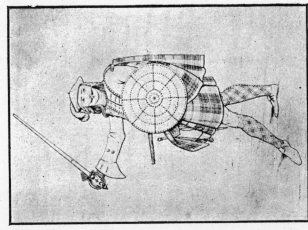

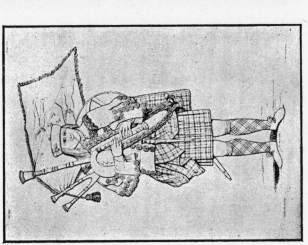

CONTEMPORARY HIGHLAND DRESS, II

(d)

(c)

though it would ease his mind. The honest man was in a sad quandary. His conscience pricked him, but he remembered the monies due to him by the Crown, and the pension and knighthood which still tarried. He thought of his daughters and his lonely old age. So he decided to stand back, wash his hands of the whole concern, and do nothing except what his official duty demanded.

Livingstone was now writing direct to Hamilton, exhorting him on January 16th not to ' trouble the Government with prisoners ' ; and on the 30th of the month we have seen that the Master wrote to Livingstone with an ominous postscript, and to Hill urging him to make the King's justice as conspicuous in the case of the MacIans as his clemency had been in other cases. But Hill was of no account now, and only Hamilton mattered. He it was who fixed the day for the attack, arranged the different parties, and selected the leaders. He seems to have been a competent soldier, ambitious to succeed in his profession, and apt to complain of slow promotion. We find both Livingstone and the Master telling him that his future depends upon how he makes use of the opportunities they offer him. The men he picked were mostly Breadalbane's own people, and, though no letters on the subject are extant, it is certain that the most heinous treachery in the business was devised by Breadalbane and ordered by Hamilton. Treachery, indeed, was, as we have seen, inherent in the plan if it was to be 'secret and sudden,' but the special form adopted was in such utter defiance of every Highland tradition that it could only have proceeded from the brain of one long destitute of honour, and have been executed by a time-serving Lowlander to whom Highlanders were no better than beasts of chase and warren. The actual operations, too, could only be entrusted to men who, body and soul, were Breadalbane's creatures.

The general scheme of netting Glencoe, though not its exact details, was known to the whole staff of the Inverlochy garrison. Hill did nothing. Two officers protested, and were put under arrest and sent prisoners to Glasgow. We do not know at what stage they made their protest, but it is possible that it was not till the actual day of the tragedy, when they were in Hamilton's company and saw the horrors with their own eyes. In that case their names were Francis Farquhar and Gilbert Kennedy.

The Jacobite journalist got an apt title for his pamphlet on Glencoe from the Emperor Gallienus, whose instructions to his ministers, after the defeat of Ingenuus in Illyricum, put Breadalbane's notions about extirpation in frank Latin. ' Non mihi satisfacies, si tantum armatos occideris, quos et fors belli interimere potuisset. Perimendus est omnis sexus virilis, si et senes atque impuberes sine reprehensione nostra occidi possent. Occidendus est quicumque male voluit . . . Lacera, occide, concide.'

On Monday the first day of February word came to Glencoe that a body of soldiers was approaching by the shore road from Balla-chulish. The news spread like wild-fire, and every MacIan who had a sword or a musket hastened to bury it deep in the peat-stacks, or in a cairn of stones, or in some cunning place in the thatch. They had the Government's protection, but they did not wish to give up their arms, without which in those lawless times they felt themselves at the mercy of any ill-wishers. Moreover, the young men had their hunting to think of. John, the chief's eldest son, with twenty MacIans in his tail, waited at the foot of the glen to find out the errand of the strangers.

He saw a force of one hundred and twenty men in red coats and grey breeks, and a glance told him that they were of Argyll's regiment. At the head strode one whom he knew well. It was a tall man, with a long thin face, a hooked nose, a small petulant mouth like a girl's, and a delicate pointed chin. He wore his own hair, which was flaxen and scarcely tinged with grey, though his age was sixty. His complexion was still youthful, but his eyes had the glazed look of one much addicted to the bottle. The man carried himself well, and at the first glance seemed a model of manly beauty ; it was only the second that showed the ravages of time and indulgence. . . . There was no mistaking their kinsman of Glenlyon.

Robert Campbell of Glenlyon had been born to a good but encumbered estate, and in his youth he had made ducks and drakes of it. He had been a notorious gambler, a heavy drinker, and something of a dandy. His political ventures, too, had been unlucky, for he had been a friend of the ill-fated Argyll who had suffered death seven years before. Bit by bit he had to sell his patrimony, till he became little more than a hanger-on of Breadalbane. Now poverty had made him a soldier, and for two years he had had a captain's commission in Argyll's regiment. He was a man, John knew, who could have no good-will to Glencoe, for had he not lost heavily in the *creagh* which MacIan and Keppoch had driven from his few remaining lands after Killiecrankie—that exploit about which Breadalbane had been so bitter at the Achallader meeting? Yet oddly enough he was kin by marriage to his brother Alasdair. His mother had taken Stewart of Appin as her third husband, and Alasdair's wife was her granddaughter, and therefore Glenlyon's niece.

The remembrance of this marriage tie was not much comfort to John, as he advanced to meet the newcomers. If the red soldiers were coming to the glen, there was no man in the world he would not have preferred as their captain.

But Glenlyon greeted him with demonstrative affection. He had always been famous for his hearty manners.

' Here's a burden come to your back, cousin,' he cried. ' It's no doing of mine, but a poor soldier must obey orders. We've been out to redd up things Invergarry way. . . . No, that affair is not finished, but the weather was unchancy and the Colonel has called a halt. Inverlochy is like a cried fair, and they are so throng that there was no house-room for my lads. So what with that, and what with this matter of the cess and hearth-money— weary fall the Parliament that is aye laying new taxes on us poor Highlandmen !—nothing would content the Colonel but he must pack us off to Glencoe. We seek only bed and bite and sup for a week or two. I know it's a heavy affliction, but I'll see that it's made as light for you as possible. If you're to have sodgers quartered on you, it's better that a friend and a kinsman should have the doing of it.'

He laid his hand on John's shoulder, a fine figure of a man, flushed with the sharp weather,

almost as tall as old MacIan himself, a trim
soldier, but a fellow-Highlander too, with his
green Campbell plaid buckled about his middle.
He spoke with an easy geniality, before which
the other's constraint melted.

'You are welcome, Glenlyon,' John said,
'you and your lads. It's not much that Glencoe has to offer, but it's all yours for the taking.'

''Deed I never doubted it,' was the answer.
'And how is the good man, your father?
And my nevoy Sandy?' He called up the
two other officers, whom he introduced as
Lieutenant Lindsay and Ensign Lindsay.
'Helen's kin,' he explained. 'Man, this is a
fair family gathering, though it's a month too
late for Hogmanay.'

The troops came to Carnoch with John and
Glenlyon walking side by side at their head.
MacIan received them with the dignity of an
erstwhile opponent, but the courtesy of a chief
and a gentleman. The men would be billeted
up and down among the cottages, and as for
the officers they were given their choice of
the principal dwellings, Carnoch, Achnacon,
Inverrigan and Achtriachtan. It seemed that
Glenlyon had already made his choice.

CAPTAIN ROBERT CAMPBELL OF GLENLYON
*(From the portrait by an unknown artist in the Scottish National
Portrait Gallery)*

'Inverrigan for me,' he cried in his hearty way. 'I'll not be putting yourself to trouble on my account, MacIan. I'll leave Achtriachtan and Achnacon, too, to the sole enjoyment of their firesides. Inverrigan is the place for us, where I'll be in the heart of my folk—and of your kind folk.'

There was a great bustle all that day allotting billets to the men and moving baggage. Glenlyon and the Lindsays dined with the chief, and the first grew merry. There was new-killed venison on the table, and mutton-ham, and salt beef from the mart; fresh oat-cakes were baked on the girdle, and MacIan set out his foreign brandy. It seemed that the Argyll men had brought few stores with them except a supply of French claret and *aqua vitae*.

'This is better than Inverlochy,' Glenlyon cried in his husky drunkard's voice. 'Here's a feast of fat things, and up yonder there was nothing but thin kale and a thrawn auld wife of a Governor.'

When the strangers had gone to their quarters, MacIan talked with his sons.

'I like it ill,' said Alasdair. 'Glenlyon never came to Glencoe for Glencoe's good. He's a

fine couthy fellow, but the word I have heard
of him is that his heart is rotten as peat ! '

'Maybe so,' said the old man. 'But he is
our guest and must be treated well. You can
sleep easy in your bed, Sandy, for now we are
doubly secure. We have the Government's
protection, and these men have eaten our salt.'

CHAPTER V

THE THIRTEENTH OF FEBRUARY

THE hundred and twenty soldiers of Argyll's were billeted among the cottages, three in one house and five in another, according to the size of the cotter's family. They were given the best entertainment the glen could offer; not very lavish since it was winter-time, but, what with kippered salmon and occasional deer-meat, better than the meagre rations of Inverlochy. Such hospitality meant that the hosts had to go very bare themselves. Glenlyon and the two Lindsays were with the tacksman at Inverrigan, but they had few meals at home. MacIan was living not at Carnoch but at his farm a little way up the stream which descends from the Bhuidhe glen, and near by the two houses of his sons John and Alasdair; at Achnacon was Achtriachtan's brother, and Achtriachtan himself, to share in the hospitable duties, often slept there. There were frequent dinner-parties and card-parties for the strangers, and almost every day Glen-lyon came to Alasdair's house to drink his morning draught, and to salute Alasdair's wife, his kinswoman.

The days passed pleasantly and the weather was kind for the time of year. Deep snow lay on the high tops and in the passes, for the December and January drifts had never melted, but in the valley itself the land was bare and dry. The Argyll men were mostly High-landers and Campbells, but there were a few Lowlanders who hung together and talked their own talk, since their lack of Gaelic kept them from much intimacy with the folk of the glen. There were regular drills, when Ser-geant Barber tried to smarten up the newer recruits, and in the afternoons there were often sports in the haugh, running and wrestling and that *camanachd* or shinty which was the game of all Gaeldom.

Of an evening, while the gentry were at the cards or a brew of toddy, the commonalty in the cottages had their own recreations. Stories and songs went round the fire, and among these well-mannered people there were adroit reticences. No word was said, no tale was told, by a MacIan which could wound the Campbell pride ; they spoke and sang of the common traditions of the Gael, and of those wars of William and James, and of William and Louis, which could be freely mentioned, since with the rank-and-file politics did not go deep. Also there was piping, mostly on the *feadan* or chanter, but sometimes a *piobaireachd* on the full set by a piper who knew his trade. Here, too, the airs were tactfully chosen. There were no tribal rants to awaken memories of the ancient feud between Clan Donald and Clan Diarmaid, and the pieces played were the classics known to all Albain, *The Macraes' March* and *A Kiss of the King's Hand*, and *Desperate Battle*, and once in a while the heart-breaking *Lament of Macruimen*. Sometimes, too, a MacIan would bow to his guests and play a sprig out of Lorn or Argyll to remind them of home.

No one of the soldiers, except the sergeant, had any notion of the purpose of their visit. They found themselves quartered in a kinder place than the Inverlochy barracks, and did not ask further questions. They were absorbed into the life of the glen as if they had been in their native clachans. The gentry, too, seemed at ease. The Lindsays were lumpish, sullen youths, but Glenlyon was a travelled man and a gentleman, a merry companion, and, when sober, very fastidious in his breeding. He would talk of politics with a shrug of his shoulders and a twinkle of his eye which precluded any danger of offence ; he had wonderful tales of his own doings and much scandal about the great ; his manner was hearty and endearing, and if in his cups he was prone to bragging, it was done with humour and good-fellowship. There was no guile in that wandering drunken eye.

So thought all except Alasdair. MacIan himself was strong on Glenlyon's simplicity. ' A rattling through-other fellow,' he said, ' whose worst foe is himself. He was never a match for yon fox of Breadalbane, so he finds himself at sixty Breadalbane's gillie. It's the queer old *bodach* he'll be in another ten years. But I tell you the man's mind is honester than sets with his tartan or his service.'

John had agreed, but Alasdair had still his doubts. Glenlyon seemed to him to be nervous

123

about something, to be waiting for something which he half feared and half hungered for. He had detected strange looks passing between him and the sullen Lindsays. Also his wife, Glenlyon's own kin, had a woman's forebodings. She would wake him in the night to question him. A cheerful soul, like all the Appin folk, she seemed now to have fallen into a strange depression of spirit.

So the life went on for eleven days, till Friday, the 12th of February. That day the weather changed. The wind shifted to the north-east, and whined through the gullies of Aonach Eagach. 'There will be snow ere evening,' said the old men ; 'in twenty-four hours the corries will be flat with the braes.'

There was a change, too, in Glenlyon's demeanour. The anxiety which Alasdair had detected in him seemed to be sharpened. There was no drilling that forenoon in the haughs ; instead he ordered a route-march and sent a half-company swinging past Carnoch along the road to Ballachulish. Alasdair had seen him in secret confabulation with Sergeant

VIEW OF GLENCOE

Photo by G. P. Abraham Ltd.

Barber ; he had also observed the sergeant talking privately to some of the soldiers, and had noted how their faces after his talk grew troubled and a little scared.

In the afternoon there were sports as usual in the meadows by Carnoch. This time they were a dismal business, for the soldiers seemed to have lost their zest for games, and the air had suddenly grown piercing cold. When Alasdair went into his house at the darkening his wife had a curious tale for him. A child had brought it, a child who had been at the sports and had watched them from beside the great boulder which some glacier long ago had brought down from the hills. The story was that a soldier, an Argyll man, had slapped the boulder with his hand and addressed it in Gaelic. ' *Grey stone of the glen,*' he had said, ' *great is your right to be here. Yet if you but knew what will happen this night, you would be up and away.*'

Alasdair tried to reassure her. ' An Argyll-man's nonsense,' he said. ' They are the lads for daft speeches. Nothing will happen this night except an on-ding of snow.' But she refused to be comforted ; she repeated the tale to others, and because of it there were many sleepless that night—to their own salvation.

In the evening Glenlyon recovered his composure. More, he was in wild spirits. He summoned John and Alasdair to Inverrigan to a card-party, and with the two Lindsays they played till supper-time. He had been bidden to dine next day by MacIan, he told them, and to bring his officers. Oddly enough he did not invite the brothers to sup with him, but dismissed them about seven o'clock. 'I have gotten news,' he said, 'news which will mean some work for me before bedtime. I fear our pleasant little family gathering is near its end. There's fresh trouble up Glengarry's way, and any hour we may have to take the road.' He was sober, but yet he had the same high laugh and uncertain eye as when he was drunk. Alasdair turned away from Inverrigan with a mind as heavy as the sky above him, from which were hurrying the first couriers of the snow.

The orders had gone out. That morning at Inverlochy, Hill, with a sad heart, had given

Hamilton the formal instructions passed on to him from the Master and Livingstone :—

' You are with four hundred of my regiment, and the four hundred of my lord Argil's regiment under the command of Major Duncanson, to march straight to Glenco, and there put in due execution the orders you have received from the Commander-in-chief.'

His one slender comfort was that he could saddle the responsibility on Livingstone, who had been in direct correspondence with Hamilton.

Hamilton the same day sent a special runner to Ballachulish, where Major Robert Duncanson was lying. Duncanson was Argyll's man, not Breadalbane's, but his troops were mostly the latter's, and included that Captain Drummond who had been in charge at Barcaldine when MacIan journeyed to Inveraray. He thus instructed Duncanson :—

' Pursuant to the Commander-in-Chief's and my Colonell's orders to me for putting in execution the service against the rebells of Glenco, wherein you, with the party of the Earle of Argile's regiment now under your command, are to be concerned. You are therefore to order your affairs so that you be

at the severall posts assigned you by seven of the
clock to-morrow morning, being Saturday, and fall
in action with them, at which I will endeavour to
be with the party from this place at the post appointed them. It will be necessary the avenues
minded by Lieut Campbell on the south side be
secured, that the old fox nor none of his cubs get
away. The orders are that none be spared, nor the
Government troubled with prisoners, which is all
I have to say to you till then.'

He added a postscript :—

' Please to order a guard to secure the ferry, and
the boats there ; and the boats must be all on this
side the ferry, after your men are over.'

Duncanson at Ballachulish completed the
chain by his orders to Glenlyon, which had
only four miles to travel :—

' You are hereby ordered to fall upon the rabelle,
the Macdonalds of Glenco, and to putt all to the
sword under seventy. You are to have a special care
that the old fox and his sones doe not escape your
hands. You are to secure all the avenues, that no
man escape. This you are to putt in execution at
five of the clock precisely. And by that time, or
very shortly after it, I will strive to be at you with a
stronger party. If I do not come to you at five, you
are not to tarry for me but to fall on. This is by the

King's special commands, for the good and safety of the countrie, that these miscreants be cutt off root and branch. See that this be put in execution, without fear or favour. Else you may expect to be dealt with as one not true to King nor countrie, nor a man fitt to carry a commission in the King's service. Expecting you will not faill in the fullfilling hereof, as you love yourselfe.'

Hamilton had fixed seven as the hour with Duncanson, but Duncanson, assuming with reason that Hamilton's part came later, had chosen five for Glenlyon's attack. The tone of his instructions to the latter suggests that he had some fear lest his sojourn among the MacIans might have blunted his zeal. It was an exact and comprehensive scheme of destruction. Against a little clan of two hundred, at the moment unarmed, and numbering only half a hundred fencible men, nine hundred and twenty regular soldiers were unleashed. Duncanson had only four miles to travel in the winter dawn to reach the foot of the glen ; Hamilton, moving through the night from Inverlochy, would, by way of Kinlochleven and the Devil's Staircase, come down on the upper end. A detachment of Argyll's men at Island Stalker would block escape through Appin, the laird of Weem was watching the Perthshire roads, and Breadalbane waited in the Glenorchy passes.

Alasdair went to bed, but not to sleep. It was his turn to be wakeful, and at last his anxiety drove him to half-dress himself and look out of doors. The snow had for the moment stopped falling, but there was promise of more in the wind, and it was bitter cold. Close to his house was an empty cottage used as a guard-room by the soldiers, and to his surprise he saw a light in it. It was just after midnight, when all should have been long in their beds. Then he heard footsteps in the snow, and several men entered the guard-room, including one who had the shape and carriage of the elder Lindsay. Much alarmed, he slipped off to his brother John's house, and woke him. John took the thing lightly and refused to move. ' They are doubling the guards,' he said, ' and a very proper course. In this devil's weather the sentries need to be relieved often. That's the reason of the extra folk in the guard-room. Glenlyon's a careful man. Back to your bed, Sandy.' Alasdair, half-frozen, returned to his own house, and presently was asleep.

By five o'clock on the morning of Saturday 13th the wind had grown to a tempest, and the snow was drifting heavily. About that hour Lieutenant Lindsay and a few soldiers presented themselves at MacIan's house, and asked civilly to see the chief on a pressing matter. They were at once admitted, and MacIan got out of bed and struggled into his trews, shouting to bring the visitors a morning draught. Suddenly two shots were fired at him from behind, one in the body and one in the brain, and the old man fell dead. Then mania seized on the murderers. Lady Glencoe —to give her the title which lairds' wives bore—had risen and dressed ; they seized her, stripped her naked, and tore the rings from her fingers with their teeth. The sound of the firing had brought some of the near-by dwellers to the house. Two were shot dead, and one, Duncan Don, who had come with letters from the Braes of Mar, was badly wounded. Lindsay and his party flung the three corpses out of doors into the snow, and the wounded man

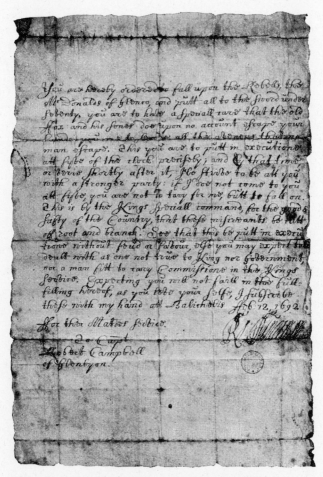

You are hereby ordered to fall upon the Rebells, the
McDonalds of Glenco, and putt all to the sword under
seventy, you are to have a spetiall care that the old
fox and his sones doe upon no account escape your
hands, you are to secure all the avenues that noe
man escape. This you are to putt in execution
att fyve of the clock precisely; and by that time
or very shortly after it, I'le strive to be att you
with a stronger party; if I doe not come to you
att fyve, you are not to tary for me, butt to fall on.
This is by the Kings speciall command, for the good &
safty of the Country, that these miscreants be cutt
off root and branch. See that this be putt in execu-
tione without feud or favour, else you may expect to
be dealt with as one not true to King nor Government,
nor a man fitt to carry Commissione in the Kings
service. Expecting you will not faill in the fullfilling hereof, as you love your selfe, I subscribe
these with my hand att Balicholis Febr 12, 1692

For their Majesties service.

R.
To Capt
Robert Campbell
of Glenlyon.

DUNCANSON'S LETTER TO GLENLYON

(From the original in the Scottish National Library)

whom they took for dead, and then turned to leave. . . . Through the drift came another party to meet them, buffeting their way up from Loch Leven. It was Duncanson and his four hundred.

The gale blanketed the sound of the shots, and the chief's sons, whose houses were a little way off, heard nothing. But it was now John who was wakeful. Before the shooting began he had heard the movement of troops outside his window; there was shouting, perhaps because some of the better disposed wished to give him the alarm. He rose, dressed, and ran to Inverrigan to find out what was happening from Glenlyon himself, apparently not dreaming of any danger to his father. He found Glenlyon up and dressed, and got a cheerful greeting. 'What's the steer?' he cried. 'The steer is that we're off to take order with Glengarry. What ails you, man? You're as white as the snow on your plaid.' Then he burst into his jolly laugh. 'Feared for Glencoe? Is it likely? Is it likely I would lift my hand against my good friends, or if I was so ill-minded that I would not first pass the word to my nevoy Sandy? Back to your bed and thank God that you have not to take the road in this hell-begotten weather.'

John went home, only half reassured, and lay down, but did not undress. He may have dozed for an hour, not more. A servant rushed in and told him that, in a pause of the snow, he had seen soldiers moving towards his door. John went out and saw not fifty yards off a party of twenty redcoats, with their bayonets screwed into their musket-barrels. He had never seen them before, for they were Duncanson's men. . . . He knew the truth at last, and fled to the snow-laden scrub below the screes of Meall Mor.

There he stumbled upon another fugitive. Alasdair ten minutes earlier had been waked by his servant, who asked him if it were a time to sleep when they were killing his brother, for he had seen the soldiers with bayonets fixed approaching John's house. That which he had long dreaded had come to pass, and Alasdair acted on a plan already formed in his head. He got his little household through the snow to a place of temporary concealment, while he himself took to the hillside. Like John he did not think of his father's

135

house, but of Inverrigan and Achnacon as
the danger-points. So he ran along the slopes
of the south wall of the glen in order to recon-
noitre, and as he ran he met his brother.
They stood and listened, for in the hollow
below was the sound of guns—many guns.
They came from Achnacon.

Sergeant Barber was busy there. Something
had happened to alarm the household, for
Achnacon himself was up and dressed, and
was sitting by the fire with Achtriachtan his
brother, and eight other men who had come
in from the cottages. Suddenly there was a
volley, and Achtriachtan fell dead, and four
more. The others dropped on the floor, all
of them wounded. Barber bent over Achnacon
and asked him if he were alive. ' I live,' was
the answer, ' and I have but the one wish—if
I must die, to die out of doors.' ' I have eaten
your bread,' said the sergeant, ' so I will do
you that kindness.' He was led outside, and
put up before the muzzles of the guns. But
Achnacon was a powerful man, and wrath and
fear made him desperate. He flung his plaid
over the soldiers' faces, broke through the
cordon, and made for the hills, while the other

four indoors managed to creep out by the back of the house. Barber made short work of those left in Achnacon hamlet. One was a child who was never seen again : only his hand was found ; he may have died in the snow and been devoured by fox or eagle. The bodies of the dead were flung on to the midden and covered with dung.

At Inverrigan was Glenlyon. John had not long left him before the work of murder began. Nine men were taken, bound hand and foot, and shot. Then he seems to have sickened of the business and inclined to hold his hand. But Captain Drummond arrived from Duncanson's party, and as Breadalbane's henchman he remembered his chief's orders. He and Barber seem to have been the most bloody-minded of the crew. Glenlyon had spared a lad of twenty. Drummond, who had the same military rank, reminded him of his instructions, and shot the youth dead. A boy of thirteen years ran out and clung to Glenlyon's knees ; Glenlyon would have saved him, but he was pistolled by Drummond. A child of four or five years was among the victims, and a woman—an excess which even Gallienus had not commanded. The bodies were hastily shovelled into shallow graves.

It was the same in all the cottages. Wherever there was a living male who could be laid hands on he died by shot or steel. Among the victims was an old man of eighty. Then, when there was no life left, the soldiers turned to other work. They loosed the cattle from the byres, the sheep from the pens, and the shelties from the rude stables. As John and Alasdair strained their ears from the skirts of Meall Mor they heard the lowing of hungry animals, who had missed their morning meal of bog-hay. And as the February dawn turned the dark into grey, they saw the driving snow redden with a glare from the valley, and knew the cause. Every cottage and hut and hovel was going up in flames.

By eight o'clock the business was over, but Glenlyon and Duncanson had not fulfilled their masters' commands. To be sure, the Government was not going to be troubled with prisoners, but they had made but a poor killing. Thirty bodies at the most, and of them several were children and at least one a woman. Most of the younger men had escaped, and though the old fox was dead his cubs were still at large. They consoled themselves by reflecting that there was but one way out of Glencoe, and that Hamilton with his Inverlochy men was stopping that bolt-hole. So they turned to their task of burning and plundering with an easy mind.

But all was not well with Hamilton. He had marched by night down the shore road from Inverlochy, and long before dawn had reached Kinlochleven. There he split up his command into parties, each with its special instructions, but all with orders to slay every man they met and make no prisoners. But on their way across the hills by the Devil's Staircase they encountered so fierce a blizzard that they were obliged repeatedly to stop and take shelter. John Forbes, Hill's major, who unwillingly accompanied them, must have thanked Heaven for the weather. What with one thing and another it was eleven in the forenoon before they found themselves at the upper end of Glencoe.

There they were met by Duncanson, who, weary of waiting, was making a patrol of the glen. He reported that old MacIan was dead and thirty-odd of his men, but that the rest had flown to the hills. Hamilton went down the river, killed an old man, burned one or two more houses, and realised that he could do nothing further. Through no fault of his own he had failed to carry out to the full the mission which was to bring him fame and fortune. His comfort was that the refugees in the hills were doomed, though they did not fall by his guns, for no human beings could live long in such a tempest of wind and ice. He contented himself with seeing to the booty, most of which would be the perquisite of the officers. The pitiful little belongings of the clan, clothes, trinkets, spoons and cups and platters, were already in the soldiers' pouches. Fatigue parties were appointed, and by the afternoon the whole stock of the glen, nine hundred cattle, two hundred horses, and a multitude of sheep and goats, were being driven across the narrows of Loch Leven on their way to Inverlochy.

Meantime what of the survivors of the little clan ? The snow was their salvation, for in five yards a man was lost to sight in the drift, and they had the advantage of knowing the ground like their own steadings. Except for a young man there were but two winter roads out of Glencoe—one by the shore to Appin, and one by the east to Rannoch and Glenorchy. The first they knew was blocked by Duncanson, but they did not know of Hamilton's purpose to net the upper end. There was a third, which an active man might manage, the pass of the Laroch between Meall Mor and Ben Vair, but there, too, Duncanson was the barrier. The only hope was to go up the glen.

One or two hunters escaped by the mountain gullies, north into Mamore, and to the Macdonald dwellings on Loch Treig. But these routes were only for the mountaineer, and many desperate miles had to be covered before a place of safety was reached. In such weather it was necessary not only to get out of the clutches of the assassins but to find food and shelter, for even the hardiest could scarcely survive a night among the blizzards and snow-wreaths of the high corries.

There was only one ultimate sanctuary—Appin—for Keppoch was too distant. In Appin there would be refuge with a friendly

141

people, a people strong enough, too, to defend the refugees. But how to get to Appin since the coast road was shut. There were two possible routes—one by the Bhuidhe glen : a second through the Lairig Gartain, between the Shepherds of Etive to Dalness ; after that the way lay down Glen Etive, where there were only shepherds' bothies, to the head of the sea-loch, and then across the low *beallach* to Glen Ure and Glen Creran. Local tradition declares that most of the people escaped by the first road, but it is certain that in winter weather it was possible only for the young and the strong. The weaker folk must have followed the second. Before it was yet light, while Glenlyon and Duncanson were burning the clachans and driving out the cattle, men, women and children, old and young, many of them half-naked, were struggling up the glen in the teeth of the storm. Once they were past Loch Triachtan they were out of the danger of the troops. The Devil's Staircase descends the northern wall opposite the opening of the Lairig Gartain, but the fugitives were inside the pass long before Hamilton appeared from Mamore.

It was a cruel journey, for the snow still drifted. There were grandfathers and grandmothers among them, women heavy with child, mothers with infants at the breast, sick folk and the very young. To their bewilderment and terror were soon added the pangs of hunger, fatigue and an extreme cold. Such as reached Dalness found temporary shelter and entertainment, for the tenant was a MacIan whom Breadalbane's men had strangely omitted to molest. But some died on the road thither, and more on the further road down the Etive or over the *beallach* to Glen Ure. Among the latter was Lady Glencoe, her fingers torn by the teeth of Lindsay's troops. Some thirty were murdered in the glen, and as many perished from the hardships of the flight. But in the end Appin was reached, and there the MacIans found roofs to cover them, and a share of Appin's scanty winter provender, and armed Stewarts to protect them should their enemies follow. In Appin the little clan was nursed back to life.

By the afternoon of the 13th Glencoe was a silent place. Scorched thatch still smoked among the snow-drifts, and ravens barked above the blood-smears on the blackened thresholds. From Aonach Eagach and Aonach Dubh the eagles and buzzards were gathering where the corpses had been left unburied. Except for these there was no sound—save that from Loch Leven shore came the far-away echo of Glenlyon's pipes. The tune they played was *The Glen is Mine*.

CHAPTER VI

THE RECKONING

GLENCOE was left to the peace of death, and
soon the snow shrouded the charred roof-trees
and the bloody hearthstones. Hamilton, Duncanson and Glenlyon reported at Inverlochy.
Their plan had somewhat miscarried, but the
MacIans were fugitives in the winter hills, and
it was predicted that the weather would complete the half-done job. That the affair had
been bungled could not be denied. The alarm
had been given by using muskets instead of cold
steel, and Hamilton had signally failed to stop
the main exit. Both Hill and Hamilton made
their reports to the Master of Stair, who could
only express a very moderate satisfaction.
' All I regret is that any of the sept got away,
and there is necessity to prosecute them to the
utmost. If they could go out of the country, I
could wish they were let slip, but they can
never do good there. Appin, who is the

heritor, should have encouragement to plant the place with other people than Macdonalds.' By way of a reward to Hill he promised to look into his money claims against the Government, and to take up the matter of the civil jurisdiction for which he had long been pressing.

But strange rumours were beginning to spread, coming from the talk, perhaps, of the more merciful among the soldiers, or by devious ways from the fugitives. By March 5 there was a story in London that the MacIans had been murdered in their beds after taking the oath ; the Master of Stair denied the latter part of the report, but not the first. In Edinburgh the rumour was more detailed. Argyll's regiment had been ordered south, and Glenlyon was in Edinburgh on his way to England. He was drinking heavily, and boasting at large in the coffee-houses. People noticed the wildness of his manner and the uncertainty of his eye, which belied his bold words. Bit by bit from his babbling the story came out. He was robustly impenitent. He declared that he and his colleagues were supplicating the Council for some special recognition of their meritorious services. ' I would do it again,' he cried. ' I would stab any man in Scotland or England, if my master the King ordered me, and never speir the cause. He who would not do that is no loyal subject.' But he was like a ' fey ' man, with a catch in the voice and sudden terrors in the face.

In April Glencoe was the chief talk of the Scottish capital. On April 12 the Paris *Gazette* published a summary of the doings there, accurate except in so far as it said that MacIan's two sons had perished with him. The Jacobites had been miraculously given new powder and shot, and they were not slow in using it. In April a pamphlet appeared in London, in the form of a letter from Scotland, which told correctly the full tale. At first its horrors were not realised, for the Jacobite journalists were fond of making people's flesh creep, and did not enjoy any very high repute for veracity. But bit by bit came confirmatory evidence, damning proofs that could not be denied, and by the summer responsible people in Edinburgh and London knew that beyond question a horrid barbarity had been committed. Argyll's regiment was now quartered at Brentford on its way to Flanders, and its private soldiers were talking. Charles Leslie, the Jacobite, went out on June 30 to see them and got the full details. Both Glenlyon and Drummond were there, and, said one of the men, ' Glencoe hangs about Glenlyon night and day, and you may see him in his face.' But William had gone to his glorious and inconclusive wars, and the fall of Namur and the preparations for Steenkirk left him no time for the trivialities of Lochaber.

Secretly during the spring the MacIans began to creep back to Glencoe. First went the young men to bury the dead and report that there was nothing stirring in the glen. Then a few of the half-burned cottages were made habitable, and when the fine weather began some cattle were brought to the haughs, the gift of kindly neighbours. John and Alasdair, who knew that Hill was not ill-disposed to them, approached him for help, and accordingly on May 3 the Scottish Privy Council authorised him to grant provisional protection—' to these persons, either in general or particularly, of all security to their persons, lands and goods, and a cessation of all acts of hostility, trouble or

148

molestation to them, upon the account of their having been in arms and rebellion against their Majesties, and to take what security he shall think meet for their living peaceably until his Majesty signifies his pleasure therein.'

It was not much of a grace, for the MacIans had no goods to protect, but it enabled them to set to work to rebuild their shattered life. On October 3, Hill, having got the royal assent, formally received Glencoe into the King's peace, Alasdair acting on behalf of the clan. Four days later he wrote to the laird of Culloden : ' The Glencoe men are abundantly civil. I have put them under my lord Argyle, and have Arkenloss' surety for them till my lord comes ; for they are now my Lord Argyle's men ; for 't was very necessary they should be under some person of power, and of honesty to the Government.' Ardkinglas throughout the whole miserable business showed himself consistently honourable and humane.

But this formal pacification, and the paradox of a Campbell becoming surety for a Macdonald, did not silence the rumours. It was

149

the interest of the Jacobites to foster them, and
even the tough conscience of seventeenth-
century Scotland was disquieted. In April
1693, Livingstone wrote to Hamilton that
' some in Parliament make a talking about the
business of Glencoe, and give out that they
design to have it examined,' and a month later
he grew seriously concerned, and told the same
correspondent that Hill must come to Edinburgh to tell all he knew. ' It is not that anybody thinks that thieving tribe did not deserve
to be destroyed, but that it should have been
done by such as were quartered amongst them,
makes a great noise. I suppose I may have
pressed it somewhat upon your Colonel, knowing how slow he was in the execution of such
things.'

It was a great noise indeed, for every
opponent of the Government was soon in full
cry, not from love of Glencoe, but from hatred
of Stair. Some honest souls had indeed been
horrified by the tale, and for humanity's sake
would fain have punished the guilty. When
the Master of Stair resigned the office of Lord
Advocate, Sir John Lauder of Fountainhall
refused to accept it unless he was permitted to

prosecute the Glencoe murderers. But the main motive was politics, not justice. The Master was too powerful not to have numberless enemies, and too passionlessly wise to have many friends among the *politiques* ; Johnston of Wariston, his colleague, was intriguing against him ; while, of the extremists, the Jacobites hated him as a traitor and the enthusiasts as the enemy of true religion.

In 1693 William, induced by his tenderhearted Queen, ordered the Lord High Commissioner, the Duke of Hamilton, to institute an inquiry into the methods used in Glencoe, of which the tales grew daily wilder. But Hamilton died, and nothing was done in that Parliament. The scuffling of kites and crows in Lochaber seemed to the King of small importance compared to the thorny ecclesiastical questions which were obtruding themselves in Parliament and General Assembly. But when the House met again in the early summer of 1695 it was clear that an inquiry would be insisted upon. William anticipated the demand, and, before leaving for the Continent, he appointed a commission, under the presidency of Tweeddale, the new High Commissioner.

After three weeks Parliament began to clamour for the report, and, though technically it should have first been submitted to William in Flanders, the agitation was so great that Tweeddale was compelled to produce it on June 24.

The commission did its work with expedition and thoroughness. It took the evidence of the chief surviving MacIans, and of other Highlanders, and it had before it the letters which had passed between the Master of Stair, Livingstone, Hill, and Hamilton. Its decisions may be briefly summarised. A great wrong had been done in not presenting MacIan's certificate of submission to the Scottish Privy Council; not a very relevant point, considering that his submission was known in London, and one probably introduced to make prejudice against the elder Stair. The Master knew about MacIan's oath, and, though aware that the King had admitted Glengarry, who was in worse case, into mercy, did not countermand the general order for a massacre. The Master's letters showed that he had interpreted ' extirpation ' in a different sense to the King, and had thereby exceeded his instructions and caused ' a barbarous murder.'

Parliament proceeded to debate the matter in detail. Hill was called before them and exonerated. A warrant was granted for the citation of Hamilton, who fled the country. The King was asked to send home for trial Major Duncanson, Captain Drummond, Lieutenant Lindsay and Sergeant Barber, who were serving in Flanders and so beyond the reach of the ordinary law. On July 10 the House in an address to the King extolled his mercy, for reasons which are not apparent, demanded the prosecution of the minor offenders from Hamilton downwards, and decided that Hill and Livingstone were covered by the orders of the Secretary of State. Then it turned to the Master, the true quarry that the hounds had always in view. 'We beg your Majesty will give such orders about him, for vindication of your Government, as you in your Royal wisdom shall think fit.'

The inquiry had been honest, but not so the findings of the commission or the resolution of Parliament. It is difficult to resist Macaulay's argument that the subordinates were covered by their military duty, and, whatever their moral guilt, were legally blameless. If this plea be disallowed, then why did not the blame attach throughout the whole hierarchy, up through Hill and Livingstone to the King ? If it be argued that the worst horror, ' murder under trust,' which especially shocked the public mind, was due to Hamilton's specific orders, it may be answered that some kind of treachery was implicit in all the orders both of Livingstone and the Master, since they insisted on quiet and secrecy, though they did not contemplate the hideous sadism of the actual deeds. It was a mere quibble which exonerated William while it condemned the Master, and a worse quibble which concentrated on the minor malefactors and did not ask for the Master's trial. Policy over-rode justice, for Parliament knew that the King would never surrender Stair, and moreover that, if he was brought to trial, that trial would be a farce without the King as a witness. No doubt it was also aware that Breadalbane stood behind the whole business, but had been too wary to leave one scrap of incriminating evidence. He was indeed arrested and sent to Edinburgh Castle for the treasonable secret clauses arranged at Achallader in June 1691, but his defence was accepted that he only arranged these clauses to get to the bottom of the Jacobite plots, and he was presently released.

William did nothing. In common decency he could do nothing, for he knew that a great part of the moral responsibility was his own. He removed the Master from the Scottish Secretaryship—he could hardly do less in view of the finding of Parliament ; and the Scottish politicians, having got their way, turned joyfully to the Darien adventure. But he gave him an indemnity, ' his Majesty being willing to pardon, forgive and remit any excess of zeal in going beyond his instructions by the said John Viscount Stair, and that he had no hand in the barbarous manner of execution' ; and as a token of his favour granted him the teinds of the regality of Glenluce in his own Galloway country.

The Jacobite hope *Qui Glencoat Glencoabitur* was never realised. Hamilton was indeed put to the horn and disappears from history, but no punishment fell on the three Lowlanders who were guilty of the worst barbarities—

155

Drummond, Lindsay and Barber. Hill got his knighthood—and, let us hope, his pension, for he was an honest if ineffectual being—but he did not live long to enjoy it. Livingstone became Viscount Teviot. Glenlyon had risen to be a colonel before he died at Bruges in August 1696. As for Breadalbane, he continued his infamies to an extreme old age. He was deep in the Jacobite attempt of 1707, and, when he was nearly eighty, he rose with Mar in the 'Fifteen, and managed to shuffle out after Sheriffmuir. He advised Mar's officers, since they were good for nothing else, to buy a printing press and start a newspaper ! The old reprobate had not one rag of virtue, but he had a sense of humour.

Of the two greater figures in the tragedy, the Master of Stair was occluded for a brief time from the service of the State. He ventured a thousand pounds in the Darien scheme, which he doubtless lost. In 1695 he succeeded his father as second viscount ; in 1702 he was a privy councillor, and in 1703 Anne made him an earl. He was the ablest Scotsman of his day—the man, said Defoe, ' of greatest counsel in the kingdom.' He was among the chief architects of the Union, but died of apoplexy at the age of fifty-nine, on the eve of its final ratification.   Unloved and unloving, careless of common esteem, he found such happiness as was permitted him in the exercise of his superb intelligence and in a cynical condescension to the follies of mankind.

As for the King, he marched resolutely upon his appointed way, through success and un-success, bereavement and broken health, till that February day in 1702 when the molehill of the ' little gentleman in black velvet,' long to be toasted by the Jacobites, brought down his horse at Hampton Court, and he died a few months after the exiled James.   William was a great man and a great European statesman, but to Scotland he meant little.   He never crossed the Border.   He had to bear much of the blame for two dismal tragedies, Glencoe and Darien.   The Edinburgh mob forced the bell-ringers of St. Giles's to play the tune of ' Wilful Willie.'   Seasons of bitter famine, for which he got the credit, coincided with his continental wars.   On the 8th of March 1702, the day of his death, a Highland widow announced to her neighbours the good tidings.

When asked how she knew, her answer was that her cow had given twice as much milk as she had had from her for seven years.

The Parliament of Scotland recommended that the survivors of Glencoe might have some reparations made to them for their losses and be supplied with the necessaries of life. Nothing was done, except that the Privy Council instructed the authorities of Argyll not to press for payment of the cess. Yet the little clan managed to creep back to a certain stability. John, as chief, drew the survivors together, and, aided by Appin and Keppoch and Glengarry, built up their shattered life. He died, after building a new house at Carnoch, and his successor was the child of two who had been carried to the hills by his nurse on the morning of the massacre. The clan would appear to have grown in numbers. In 1745 Duncan Forbes, the Lord President, put the fighting men at one hundred and fifty, and the report of the minister of Inverness a year later rated them at one hundred. Better seasons and the growing wealth of the Lowlands had no doubt improved the trade in black cattle and skins and increased their means of livelihood.

There was to be one final drama in the story of the glen before the broken lights of its past faded into common day. The chief, Alasdair, and his twin brothers, James and Donald, rose in the 'Forty-five. They joined Prince Charles Edward on August 27 with one hundred and twenty men ; Alasdair was a member of the Prince's Council and fought in all his battles. After Culloden he was attainted, and lay some years in prison, but he was alive in the glen in 1773. The high moment of the MacIans was in the march to Edinburgh, when the Prince's army occupied Linlithgow. Near by stood the house of Newliston, a Stair dwelling which the Master had got in virtue of his wife. Alasdair demanded that his men and no others should guard Newliston, that they might prove to the world that the purity of the cause for which they fought was smirched by no ' vileinye of hate.'

The last word—and a great word—was with Glencoe.

NOTES

THE principal authority for the massacre of Glencoe is the report of the inquiry by the Commission of the Scottish Parliament, presented in June 1695. It was published as a pamphlet by B. Bragg, 'at the Blue Ball in Ave-Mary-Lane,' in 1703, and it is reprinted in Howell's *State Trials*, vol. xiii., in *Somers Tracts*, vol. xi., and in *Highland Papers*, 99-116.

The first account of the affair was given in a pamphlet published in 1692, 'A Letter from a Gentleman in Scotland, to his Friend at London, who desired a particular account of the Business of Glenco.' This was reissued, with a commentary, in *Gallienus Redivivus, or Murder Will Out*, in 1695, after the publication of the Parliamentary Commission's report. *Gallienus Redivivus*, whose author was Charles Leslie, the Jacobite pamphleteer (for whom see *D.N.B.*), was reprinted in *Miscellanea Scottica* (Glasgow, 1820), vol. iii. In the same year appeared a second pamphlet, also in *Somers Tracts*, which was partly a defence of the Master of Stair,— 'An Impartial Account of some of the Transactions in Scotland, concerning the Earl of Breadalbane, Viscount and Master of Stair, Glenco-men, Bishop of Galloway, and Mr. Duncan Robertson. In a Letter to a Friend.'

The other contemporary authorities are the *Leven and Melville Papers* (Bannatyne Club, 1843); *Papers Illustra-*

NOTES

*tive of the Political Condition of the Highlands of Scotland
from 1689-1696* (Maitland Club, 1845) ; *Culloden Papers*
(1815) ; *Memoirs of Locheill* (Abbotsford and Maitland
Clubs, 1842) ; *Memoirs of Hugh Mackay* (Bannatyne Club,
1833) ; Mackay, *Life of Hugh Mackay* (Bannatyne Club,
1836) ; John Macky, *Memoirs of Secret Services* (1733 ;
and Roxburghe Club, 1895) ; *Lockhart Papers* (1817) ;
and *Memoirs of Great Britain and Ireland, 1681-92*, by
Sir John Dalrymple of Cranstoun (3 vols., 1790).

The story has been retold by all the modern historians
of Scotland, such as Hill Burton, Hume Brown, and
Andrew Lang—by the last most judicially. It is also
the subject of one of Macaulay's most famous chapters,
which has been controverted, and partly corrected, by
John Paget in his *Paradoxes and Puzzles* (1874), 33-76.

In my boyhood in Appin I used to hear local legends ;
but their evidence is scarcely to be trusted, for Glencoe
became almost at once a literary theme, and the local
traditions must have been coloured and supplemented
from outside sources. The topography is based on my
own stalking and mountaineering recollections.

I

p. 16, l. 6. *Highland Papers*, 3, 8.
p. 16, l. 25. *Ibid.*, 10.
p. 17, l. 15. For Monk's methods, see Firth, *Scotland and
the Protectorate*, xxxvi., etc. ; Thurloe, *State
Papers*, iii. 497, 522 ; iv. 129, 401. In
April 1656 Hill wrote from Ruthven :—
' The business prospers so well in our
hands as Justice of peace in these High-

lands that I hope in short time we may contend for civility with the Lowlands. A loose or broken man or a stranger cannot pass without a sufficient testimonial under the hand of some officer of the army or Justice of the peace ; fornicators are startled at the punishment some have received, and drunkards begin to look towards sobriety, and swearers to speak more deliberately ' (*Clarke MSS.*, xxviii. 22). There is a plan of Monk's fort among the Clarke Papers in Worcester College Library. Correspondence between Hill and Glencairn in 1654 will be found in Gwynne, *Military Memoirs* (1822), App.

p. 17, l. 20. *Clarke MSS.*, xxx. 176.

p. 17, l. 23. Mackay, *Memoirs*, 90 ; *Mem. of Locheill*, 154, 167.

p. 18, l. 9. *Leven and Melville Papers*, 415-16 ; *Highland Papers*, 88 ; *Culloden Papers*, 22.

p. 18, l. 24. Mackay, *Memoirs*, 188 ; *MS. History of Family of Buchan* by James, 16th Earl of Caithness.

p. 19, l. 4. *Culloden Papers*, 22.

p. 19, l. 6. *Leven and Melville Papers*, 522.

p. 19, l. 10. *Mem. of Locheill*, 354-5.

p. 19, l. 11. *Highland Papers*, 88.

p. 19, l. 19. Mackay, *Memoirs*, 98-9.

p. 19, l. 25. He had pressed the erection of a fort on the Government before Killiecrankie. *Life of Mackay*, 36.

p. 20, l. 19. *Ibid.*, 178.

p. 20, l. 24. Mackay, *Memoirs*, 341, 354 ; *Life of Mackay*, 183 ; *Leven and Melville Papers*, 477.

p. 21, l. 7. *Life of Mackay*, 176.

p. 21, l. 8. *Cal. S.P. Dom. (1690-1)*, 48.

p. 21, l. 9. Hill found them ' brutish ' and mutinous. *Leven and Melville Papers*, 496-7.

p. 21, l. 16. *Highland Papers*, 6.

p. 24, l. 10. *Life of Mackay*, 84-8 ; *Leven and Melville Papers*, 435, 442.

p. 26, l. 9. *Lockhart Papers*, i. 63.

p. 26, l. 13. *Highland Papers*, 46.

p. 27, l. 5. ' He was the merriest grave man I ever saw, and no sooner was told anybody's name than he had some pleasant thing to say of him, mocked the while, and had a way of laughing inwardly.'—Master of Sinclair, *Memoirs*, 185. ' He is as cunning as a fox ; wise as a serpent ; but as slippery as an eel. No Government can trust him, but where his own private interest is in view.'—John Macky, *Memoirs of Secret Services*, 119.

p. 28, l. 3. Mackay, *Memoirs*, 83.

p. 28, l. 4. *Life of Mackay*, 84.

p. 28, l. 6. *Leven and Melville Papers*, 421-3.

p. 28, l. 15. Forbes's plan is in *Culloden Papers*, 14-18 ; Breadalbane's, which anticipated Chatham's famous policy, is in *Highland Papers*, 53-6, and Dalrymple, *Memoirs*, Pt. ii., Bk. vi., App. 218-22.

p. 30, l. 12. *Leven and Melville Papers*, 613, etc. ; *Highland Papers*, 10, etc.

p. 30, l. 14. This apparently was the Master of Stair's doing. *Highland Papers*, 18.

p. 31, l. 2. *Ibid.*, 21-2 ; *Culloden Papers*, 18-19.

p. 31, l. 6. *Highland Papers*, 21-2, 40.

p. 31, l. 14. There is no reason to accept the general belief that Breadalbane embezzled public funds granted him for the pacification. I cannot find that he ever got any, and what money he spent seems to have come out of his own pocket. See Dalrymple to Hill, *Highland Papers*, 76.

p. 31, l. 18. *Leven and Melville Papers*, 650.

p. 31, l. 25. *Highland Papers*, 35-8.

p. 32, l. 11. *Ibid.*, 52.

p. 32, l. 19. *Ibid.*, 15.

p. 32, l. 22. *Gallienus Redivivus*, 44.

p. 33, l. 4. *Highland Papers*, 31.

p. 33, l. 18. Lochiel actually reached Inveraray on December 31. *Mem. of Locheill.*

p. 34, l. 7. *Culloden Papers*, 13.

p. 35, l. 22. *Life of Mackay*, 156, 174.

p. 35, l. 26. Dalrymple, *op. cit.*, 217 ; *Highland Papers*, 53.

p. 38, l. 3. Browne, *Hist. of the Clans*, ii. 183.

p. 38, l. 6. *Mem. of Locheill*, 283.

p. 38, l. 20. *Report of Parl. Comm.* ; *State Trials*, xiii. 897.

p. 38, l. 22. Firth, *Scotland and the Protectorate*, xxxvi.

p. 39, l. 3. *Highland Papers*, 23.

p. 39, l. 16. *Ibid.,* 11, 14, 16, 25, 32.

p. 41, l. 3. *Mem. of Locheill,* 322.

p. 41, l. 12. *Ibid.,* 322. He is described in the *Grameid* as 'Horridus et bibulo contectus pectore tergo.'

p. 41, l. 15. Hill Burton, *Hist. of Scotland,* vii. 400 *n.* ; Napier, *Memorials of Dundee,* iii. 625.

p. 43, l. 21. Duncan Campbell, *Lairds of Glenlyon* (1886). A list is given there of the plunder taken in this *creagh* of 1689.

p. 47, l. 14. Mackenzie, *Hist. of the Macdonalds and Lords of the Isles* (1881) ; *Historical Account of the Macdonalds of Clanranald* (1819) ; *Notes and Queries,* 6th ser., vol. x. 212.

p. 48, l. 15. Hill Burton, vii. 404 *n*

II

p. 54, l. 9. *New Statistical Account of Scotland : Argyll,* 493 *n.*

p. 56, l. 25. *State Trials,* xiii. 899 *n.*

p. 58, l. 6. *Report of Parl. Comm.*

p. 59, l. 17. *Ibid.*

p. 59, l. 20. Argyll knew on January 11, that is five days afterwards, that MacIan had been too late in taking the oath (*Highland Papers,* 62), and he could not have got word in the time except by an express message sent direct from Inveraray.

p. 60, l. 23. *Report of Parl. Comm.*

p. 62, l. 9. *Highland Papers,* 36.

III

p. 65, l. 24. Scott, introd. to *Bride of Lammermuir*; Crockett, *Scott Originals*, 244, etc.

p. 66, l. 10. Omond, *Lord Advocates of Scotland*, i. 225, etc.

p. 67, l. 2. *Lockhart Papers*, i. 88, etc. ; Macky, *Memoirs of Secret Services*, 212.

p. 67, l. 4. Balcarres, *Memoirs*, 59.

p. 71, l. 9. All through the older Scottish literature we find this traditional dislike. The 'makars' are unwearying in their savage gibes at the Highlands, and the beautiful Celtic folk-lore is a usual ingredient of their broadest farce. Cf. Sir David Lyndsay's *The Thrie Estaitis*, Pt. i., and Dunbar's *Ane Littell Interlud* (ed. Scottish Text Society), ii. 315 ; John Major, *History of Greater Britain* ; and for the late seventeenth century William Cleland's satires.

p. 71, l. 18. Dalrymple, *op. cit.*, 217.

p. 76, l. 6. *Ibid.*, 211.

p. 76, l. 7. *Ibid.*, 211.

p. 76, l. 10. *Leven and Melville Papers*, 631.

p. 76, l. 18. Dalrymple, 213 ; *Highland Papers*, 45-6.

p. 78, l. 3. Dalrymple, 215.

p. 78, l. 16. *Highland Papers*, 49.

p. 79, l. 2. *Ibid.*, 49 ; Dalrymple, 217.

p. 79, l. 22. Dalrymple, 217 ; *Highland Papers*, 51-2.

p. 80, l. 4. *Highland Papers*, 53.

p. 81, l. 26. *Ibid.*, 57-8.

p. 83, l. 13. *Ibid.*, 58-9.

p. 84, l. 10. *Ibid.*, 60-2.

p. 86, l. 22. *Ibid.*, 65 ; *Culloden Papers*, 19.

p. 87, l. 6. *Highland Papers*, 66.

p. 87, l. 15. *Ibid.*, 67.

p. 87, l. 26. *Ibid.*, 70.

p. 88, l. 3. *Ibid.*, 71.

p. 88, l. 19. *Report of Parl. Comm.*

p. 88, l. 21. See under 'Macgregor,' in Indexes to vols. vi., vii. and viii. of the *Privy Council Register*.

p. 88, l. 23. *Acts of Parl. of Scotland*, v. 398.

p. 88, l. 24. There were instances after 1692, when a laird of MacIntosh was granted letters against Macdonald of Keppoch, and Atholl against Simon Fraser of Beaufort. Hill Burton, vii. 413-14.

p. 89, l. 4. Cf. *Mem. of Locheill*, 372. In certain special cases the warrant went further, as in the grant to the Earl of Moray in 1528 to deal with Clan Chattan : 'To invade them to their utter destruction, by slaughter, burning, drowning, or other ways, and leave no creature living of that clan except priests, women and bairns.'—*Spalding Club Miscellany*, ii. 84.

p. 90, l. 24. *Report of Parl. Comm.* Burnet (*Hist. of Own Times*, ed. 1734, ii. 89) attributes the proposal for the massacre to Breadalbane, and on this point his evidence is good.

p. 92, l. 10. Burnet, *op. cit.*, ii. 89.

IV

p. 95, l. 16. Bidean nam Bian means 'the pinnacle of the skins,' a nonsensical name. The true name is almost certainly Bidean nam Beann, 'the pinnacle of the peaks.'

p. 99, l. 8. Macfarlane, *Geographical Collections* (Scot. Hist. Soc.), ii. 157.

p. 99, l. 12. Mrs. Grant of Laggan, *Letters from the Mountains* (ed. 1804), i. 83.

p. 99, l. 26. *Mem. of Locheill*, 322.

p. 102, l. 8. Grant, *Soc. and Econ. Development of Scotland before 1603*, 528.

p. 103, l. 20. Gregory, *Hist. of the Western Highlands*, 59, 412.

p. 104, l. 3. Grant, *op. cit.*, 513.

p. 104, l. 5. *Clanranald MSS.* in *Reliquiae Celticae*, ii. 181.

p. 105, l. 2. If a stag is killed to-day in Coire Gabhail it must be cut in pieces before it can be removed, so precipitous is the only outlet.

p. 105, l. 24. *Highland Papers*, 163.

p. 107, l. 26. *Report of Parl. Comm.*

p. 110, l. 12. *Highland Papers*, 69.

p. 110, l. 18. *Ibid.*, 71.

p. 111, l. 1. *Ibid.*, 48-9, 69.

p. 111, l. 24. *Gallienus Redivivus*, 48.

p. 112, l. 4. *Report of Parl. Comm.*

p. 112, l. 8. See Gibbon, *Decline and Fall* (ed. Bury), i. 275, etc.

p. 112, l. 24. *Gallienus Redivivus*, 45.

p. 114, l. 2. The ordinary account makes Alasdair's wife a daughter of Glenlyon's sister, who married a Macgregor, and one of whose sons was Rob Roy (*Highland Papers*, 105 *n.*). But it would appear that it was Glenlyon's mother who married Patrick Roy Macgregor, and that Alasdair married her granddaughter by her third husband. See Campbell, *Lairds of Glenlyon*.

p. 116, l. 14. Glenlyon married Helen Lindsay. The young men were either her nephews or cousins.

V

p. 120, l. 4. *Gallienus Redivivus*, 43.

p. 120, l. 15. The tradition in Glencoe has always been that MacIan at the time of the massacre was not living at Carnoch, but, for economy's sake, at a smaller house some way up Gleann Leac-nam-Bhuidhe, and on this point tradition is likely to be right.

p. 121, l. 5. *Report of Parl. Comm.*

p. 128, l. 8. *Highland Papers*, 73 ; *Culloden Papers*, 20.

p. 128, l. 15. Hill Burton (*op. cit.*, vii. 404 *n.*) suggests that Duncanson may have been the procurator-fiscal of Argyll himself, and this view is strengthened by a comparison of the handwriting of the order to Glenlyon with specimens of the procurator-fiscal's signature in the Scottish Record Office. There is no reason why one of the chief officers of Argyll's justiciary should not have held a high command in Argyll's regiment.

p. 129, l. 8. *Gallienus Redivivus* has after 'spared,' 'for seventy, of the sword.'

p. 129, l. 14. *Highland Papers*, 74 ; *Culloden Papers*, 20 ; *Gallienus Redivivus*, 43.

p. 130, l. 8. *Highland Papers*, 72-3 ; *Culloden Papers*, 20-21 ; *Gallienus Redivivus*, 42. Copies in *Wodrow MSS.*, and in General Register House, Edinburgh. What may well be the original has been presented to the National Library of Scotland by a Macdonald, the present Prime Minister of Britain.

p. 132, l. 3. *Gallienus Redivivus*, 47. The story given there of the eavesdropping cannot be reconciled with the evidence before the Parliamentary Commission.

p. 134, l. 2. The details of the massacre rest entirely upon the statements of the survivors, which were accepted by the Parliamentary Commission. These may be taken as true, since they were never questioned, though all the perpetrators of the murders were alive at the time.

p. 140, l. 21. The details are from the evidence taken by the Parliamentary Commission.

p. 143, l. 14. *Gallienus Redivivus*, 45.

VI

p. 146, l. 2. *Highland Papers*, 75.

p. 146, l. 15. *Ibid.*, 75.

p. 147, l. 5. *Gallienus Redivivus*, 49.

p. 148, l. 7. *Ibid.*, 50.

p. 149, l. 5. *Highland Papers*, 83.

p. 149, l. 11. *Ibid.*, 85-6.

p. 149, l. 19. *Ibid.*, 87 ; *Culloden Papers*, 22.

p. 149, l. 22. Ardkinglas's bond of surety for John and Alasdair and the young Achtriachtan is in the Inveraray archives.

p. 150, l. 17. *Highland Papers*, 90.

p. 151, l. 1. The only authority for this refusal is said to be an anonymous note scribbled on a pamphlet in the National Library of Scotland (Omond, *Lord Advocates*, i. 242 n.). But it is referred to in a poem by Robert Blair (author of *The Grave*) in Sir Thomas Dick Lauder's ' Genealogical Rolls.' See Fountainhall's *Journal* (Scot. Hist. Soc.), xxvii.

p. 151, l. 11. Macaulay, *Hist. of England* (ed. Firth), v. 2508.

p. 152, l. 5. *Acts of Parl. of Scotland*, ix. *passim*.

p. 152, l. 26. The report is in *Highland Papers*, 99-116.

p. 153, l. 3. *Acts of Parl. of Scotland*, ix. 408.

p. 153, l. 9. *Ibid.*, ix. 421-2.

p. 153, l. 20. *Ibid.*, ix. 424-5. A defence of the Master was at once issued, written by his brother, Hew Dalrymple, and it was replied to at length by the Lord Advocate, Sir James Stuart, *Highland Papers*, 120-4 ; Omond, *Lord Advocates*, i. 260.

p. 155, l. 4. *Acts of Parl. of Scotland*, ix. 366 ; Burnet, *op. cit.*, ii. 157.

p. 155, l. 20. *Highland Papers*, 143-4.

p. 155, l. 21. *Gallienus Redivivus*, 64.

p. 156, l. 7. Campbell, *Lairds of Glenlyon*.

p. 156, l. 14. Lang, *Hist. of Scotland*, iv. 212.

p. 156, l. 25. *History of the Union.*

p. 158, l. 3. This was in Glen Lyon, among a clan inclined to William's side.

p. 158, l. 7. *Highland Papers*, 149.

p. 158, l. 10. *Ibid.*, 150.

p. 158, l. 20. Stewart of Garth, *Manners and Customs of the Highlanders*, App.

p. 159, l. 10. *Itinerary of Prince Charles Edward* (Scot. Hist. Soc.), 9, 17 *n.*

p. 159, l. 12. Mrs. Grant of Laggan, *Letters from the Mountains*, i. 82, 90. The authoress was at school with his granddaughters.

p. 159, l. 22. Lang, *Prince Charles Edward*, 88 ; *State Trials*, xiii. 894 *n.*

INDEX

173